They don't speak our language

Explorations in Language Study
General Editors
Peter Doughty   Geoffrey Thornton

THEY DON'T SPEAK
OUR LANGUAGE
Essays on the language world of children and adolescents

Edited by
Sinclair Rogers

EDWARD ARNOLD

First published 1976
by Edward Arnold (publishers) Ltd
25 Hill Street, London W1X 8LL

ISBN 0 7131 0024 9

Explorations in Language Study

Language in the Junior School
E. Ashworth

Language and Community
E. A. Doughty and P. S. Doughty

Language Study, the Teacher and the Learner
P. S. Doughty and G. M. Thornton

Language, Brain and Interactive Processes
R. S. Gurney

Explorations in the Functions of Language
M. A. K. Halliday

Learning How to Mean: Explorations in the Development of Language
M. A. K. Halliday

English as a Second and Foreign Language
B. Harrison

Language in Bilingual Communities
D. Sharp

Language, Experience and School
G. M. Thornton

Accent, Dialect and the School
Peter Trudgill

Printed in Great Britain by Butler & Tanner Ltd
Frome and London

General Introduction

In the course of our efforts to develop a linguistic focus for work in English language, which was published as *Language in Use*, we came to realize the extent of the growing interest in what we would call a linguistic approach to language. Lecturers in Colleges and Departments of Education see the relevance of such an approach in the education of teachers. Many teachers in schools and in colleges of Further Education recognize that 'Educational failure is primarily *linguistic* failure', and are turning to Linguistic Science for some kind of exploration and practical guidance. Many of those now exploring the problems of relationships, community or society, from a sociological or psychological point of view wish to make use of a linguistic approach to the language in so far as it is relevant to these problems.

We were conscious of the wide divergence between the aims of the linguist, primarily interested in describing language as a system for organizing 'meanings', and the needs of those who now wanted to gain access to the insights that resulted from that interest. In particular, we were aware of the wide gap that separated the literature of academic Linguistics from the majority of those who wished to find out what Linguistic Science might have to say about language and the use of language.

Out of this experience emerged our own view of that much-used term, 'Language Study', developed initially in the chapters of *Exploring Language*, and now given expression in this series. Language Study is not a subject, but a process, which is why the series is called *Explorations in Language Study*. Each exploration is focused upon a meeting point between the insights of Linguistic Science, often in conjunction with other social sciences, and the linguistic questions raised by the study of a particular aspect of individual behaviour or human society.

5

The volumes in the series have a particular relevance to the role of language in teaching and learning. The editors intend that they should make a basic contribution to the literature of Language Study, doing justice equally to the findings of the academic disciplines involved and the practical needs of those who now want to take a linguistic view of their own particular problems of language and the use of language.

Peter Doughty
Geoffrey Thornton

Contents

ACKNOWLEDGEMENTS

The Publisher wishes to thank the following for permission to reproduce copyright material:

The Essex Music Group, Pete Townshend and Fabulous Music Ltd for two stanzas from 'My Generation' (Pete Townshend composition); MacMillan Publishing Co. Inc., New York for an extract from *The Violent-Gang* by Lewis Yablonsky (© Lewis Yablonsky 1962) and Penguin Books Ltd for short extracts and a Table from Susie Daniel and Pete McGuire (eds) *The Paint House: Words from an East End Gang* (Penguin Education Specials 1972).

Introduction

Although the primary aim of this collection of essays is to look at aspects of the ways in which language is used and the functions it has in the life and culture of children *outside* school, the first essay is an attempt to link the language required for schooling and the actual language of children. A great deal of children's time nowadays up until they are sixteen or so is spent in the formally organized and highly structured learning situation of the classroom at school. Clearly the children can and do learn a great deal about the academic studies for which schools are best geared, but the job of imparting knowledge, never an easy one, is made more difficult by the sometimes differing language and culture of the teachers and the taught.

Children come to school already having views and opinions of their own. How do children of all ages learn about the myriad of different items that make up their life and childhood culture—food, toys, TV, games, myths, music, sex, the attitudes and prejudices of adults and so on? How does a language help the child to produce in himself a 'world view' which is more or less typical of his age group? How do they learn about the great mass of the world outside the school without actually being taught about it? How do children deal with and understand the conflicts between the culture of school and that of the peer group in the outside world? On this last point the essays by Rutherford and Adelman in this collection have some valuable things to say.

Language is the critical medium through which young minds are moulded: the means by which the attitudes of the parents are passed on to the child. But the child is also an explorer, on his own in the world, using language in a variety of ways, as a method of exchanging information, gaining information, understanding society and people. The list is almost endless. A function of this

9

collection of essays is to attempt to explain the place of language in the process of acquiring knowledge and experience of social relationships, and the changing culture of childhood. The Opies' *Lore and Language of Schoolchildren* (1959) makes the point very forcibly that the language of children plays an important role in the creation of a separate childhood culture which is both changing as it interacts with the more adult culture, and, at the same time, is a part of a very strong historical tradition. This apparent dichotomy can only really be explained by the way that language acts in society, for language as a medium can be said simultaneously to conserve and alter a tradition.

Children's language as it relates to the learning situations in schools is, and has been, the subject of many books and research projects, of which the latest one: The Bullock Report 'A language for life' (DES, HMSO February 1975) stresses the critical nature of language in education. A common denominator in all these books and reports is a determination to understand the roles and functions of language in these highly structured, and in a sense artificial, situations so that learning can be enhanced.

No one would deny that outside the school adults can still deliberately use language to achieve certain effects in children, or that learning can go on outside the school gate, but much less time has been given for research in this area, and consequently we know relatively little about how language works outside of school. There are, though, differences between the inside and the outside of school:

(*a*) the school is and remains an institution of state and is seen—perhaps only dimly—by many children as a proselytizing agency run by adults trained for the job;

(*b*) the amount of overt and covert control given by the teacher;

(*c*) the formality of the social structure within the classroom clearly defining and separating the status and roles of the teacher from those of the children.

These differences between the world and the language of the child in school and outside school might be stated as differences between the levels of formality of relationships, and the amount of prior planning needed to achieve desired ends.

Language is seen as one of the major components in the achievement by the child of an understanding of the world and a holding of a set of values, as well as a tool in the communicative act of

10

learning. Thus, with so many roles for language to play in so many different scenarios as far as the child is concerned, it is as well to begin by examining some views about the nature of language itself.

Sinclair Rogers

1 The language of children and adolescents and the language of schooling

SINCLAIR ROGERS

Rival Views of Language

Over recent years there has come a deluge of books and articles on language which have had great significance to education. But the writers seem to be saying a number of contradictory things; on the one hand from Chomsky there has been the case put very strongly on theoretical grounds that any child, almost entirely irrespective of his intelligence, can and does acquire a maternal language. And use it. Lenneberg, working with severely subnormal children has supported this view; he has found, for example that

'the ability to acquire language is a biological development that is relatively independent of that elusive property called intelligence.'

Lenneberg 1966, p. 78

On the other hand, writers such as Bernstein express the view that whatever the theoretical potential for acquiring language is, some children have available to them a language which is significantly reduced in vocabulary and structures when compared with other children of the same age.

Chomsky's view is one of seeing children as active linguists working out for themselves, from the mass of primary language data that surrounds them, a set of rules or hypotheses which gradually conforms more and more to an adult speaker's internalized grammar. And to stress the point, Chomsky says that this ability to acquire a maternal language is innate in all humans.

Apart from the powerful thrust on linguistic theory of Chomsky's views, he has influenced the thinking on children's language in at least two other ways. He has successfully countered the opinion held by many that certain groups (mainly low social status groups) of children were *unable* to acquire and use the grammar of their maternal language. His other influence has been to deny the significance of the behaviourist or stimulus-response-reinforcement approach to language learning, in the course of which the techniques of imitation and practice play an important role. In so denying the behaviourist school of language acquisition, Chomsky re-affirmed the essentially creative nature of each child's individual process of language acquisition. However, the innate nature of the acquisition process is re-emphasized because of the overwhelmingly regular patterns of acquisition of language, irrespective of what sort of society the child is born into, or what maternal language he hears around him.

A child's language is not simply a copy—and a bad one at that—of adult's language. The language is rather the child's actual creation by using rules of grammar of his own design. If it is possible to sum up the two approaches of behaviourism and of Chomsky to language acquisition, it would be to say that the behaviourist sees child language as adult language filtered through a great deal of cognitive noise with the further disability of a small vocabulary. Chomsky, however, has stressed that we ought to look upon a child as a fluent speaker of his own exotic language with an ability to produce and to understand an indefinitely large number of new or novel sentences. The behaviourist view about language appears to enjoy enormous currency in schools probably because much of the learning theory given in teacher training is behaviourist. For this reason, it has been worth stressing Chomsky's position on the creativity of children's language.

●

Communicative Competence

But by concentrating on an 'idealized speaker-hearer' context, Chomsky has been criticized for ignoring the communicative aspects of using language. In acquiring a maternal language a child needs to acquire a grammar in conjunction with a competence to communicate, or, as Hymes has termed it, 'a communicative competence', for as he explains:

'We have then to account for the fact that a normal child acquires knowledge of sentences, not only as grammatical, but also as appropriate. He or she acquires competence as to when to speak, when not, and as to what to talk about with whom, when, where, in what manner. In short, a child becomes able to accomplish a repertoire of speech acts, to take part in speech events, and to evaluate their accomplishment by others. This competence, moreover, is integral with attitudes, values, and motivations concerning language, its features and uses, and integral with competence for, and attitudes toward, the interrelation of language with the other code of communicative conduct.'

Hymes 1971, pp. 277-8

What Hymes leaves undiscussed, and thus undecided, is a live issue in any consideration of the role of language in education: namely that it is believed that a particular social class habitually employs a set of communicative competences which are generally unused to carrying certain types of message. Furthermore, these types of message are expected in school, prized even, and also form the backbone medium to testing techniques and examinations. Important here, too, is the effect on a teacher a child's language dialect has, for recent research has shown that a teacher's view of a child's progress at school or, perhaps more significantly, his view of what to expect from the child, is much influenced by that child's manipulation of the language of schooling.

Failure in Schools

In much research, language has been isolated as a main contributor to educational failure, especially educational failure which is correlated with low social class. Professor Halliday has said:

'... the most immediately accessible cause of educational failure is to be sought in language. Beyond this, and underlying the linguistic failure, is a complex pattern of social and familial factors whose significance has been revealed by Bernstein's work. But while the limitations of a child's linguistic experience may ultimately be ascribed—though not in any simple or obvious way— to features of the social background, the problem as it faces the teacher is essentially a linguistic problem. It is a limitation on the child's control over the relevant functions of language in their adaptation to certain specific demands.'

Halliday 1969, in Halliday 1973, p. 19

The debate about educational failure through linguistic failure has tended to centre on two explanations of the problems with the language of schooling which it is suggested that lower working class (LWC) children have. Either LWC children have acquired *less* language than their peers from other social groups, or they have acquired a *different* language which does not include in its

15

dialects the language of schooling. The less language explanation says that the LWC child simply has less language—less vocabulary, fewer structures—than his peers; the different language explanation emphasizes language differences, especially grammatical structures, when compared with the language of the school. It must be said, though, that Cazden (1970) has argued strongly that there are inadequacies in the 'less language/different language' characterization, not least because we cannot assume that a child acquires only one way of speaking, and uses it to the same extent on every possible communicative occasion.

The Work of Bernstein

Bernstein has had great influence in educational debates in Western society. His views have gained wide acceptance in education even though certain criticisms of lack of methodology, internal inconsistency, prejudice, and so on (Labov 1969, Coulthard 1969, Rosen 1972) may appear to some to be overwhelming. The relative ease with which Bernstein can be misunderstood by even the most well-intentioned reader may partly explain why his work occupies a pre-eminent position in the literature of deprivation and in much of the educational practice and planning arising therefrom. A further explanation for this apparent power may lie in the fact that any person of good intention will see that LWC children in school very often do appear to have not only a different language from that expected in school, but also a poorer one. Many of the critics of Bernstein comment on this feature. They suggest that the situations in which Bernstein and his associates collected their data were situations in which the LWC child nearly always does less well, produces less language than his MC counterpart. As Cazden (1970) has shown, the actual situation can be the single most powerful factor in language performance. And it is regrettable that so little of the actual data appears in the published work of Bernstein and his associates. Too often they prefer to give an artificially constructed example as in Hawkins (1969) reprinted in Bernstein (1973, p. 86).

Although Bernstein is by training and experience a sociologist, from an early date he saw language as a determining factor in the relationship between educational failure and social class. It is interesting to note that he stratified society primarily in his 1965 paper by the length and quality of the person's education. This paper, 'A sociolinguistic approach to social learning', gives language a binary distinction between 'public' language which was

16

later to turn into restricted code, and 'formal' language which became later on elaborated code. The original terms were clearly an unfortunate choice of words because 'public' language was in fact the language used by enclosed groups in some privacy, although it might be said to be the language used by the public, the public of the public bar. The term 'formal' language encompassed the total stylistic range of language from formal to complete informality, at least as far as the syntax was concerned. The terms formal and public were dropped in later papers, and in the process became refined and extended. A major change which took place was that at least one other factor was added to the list of defining characteristics. This factor, which dealt with the amount of meaning potential the two types of language codes made more possible, added another dimension to the almost entirely syntactic criteria used previously.

It is these various formulations of the defining characteristics of the two language codes which have become part of the folklore of the teacher, as Rosen (1972) puts it. For this reason at least, it is worth re-stating them briefly:

Restricted code language may be characterized by fairly simple syntax which leads to a high level of structural predictability. Elaborated code language employs a more complex syntax and thus has a lower level of structural predictability and also employs a wider varying vocabulary. These are entirely linguistic features and are thus able to be verified empirically. They have, however, a wider psychological significance in that the restricted code language may facilitate a highlighting of the common denominators in unrelated situations whereas the elaborated code language may facilitate a critical awareness of the differences in unrelated situations.

Bernstein has stressed that the users of the restricted code assume a high degree of shared contexual experience between them, and so their language will exhibit a high degree of elliptical utterances and a high level of use of contextualized pronouns (see Hawkins' paper in Bernstein 1973). The users of the elaborated code do not assume, necessarily, a high degree of shared contextual experience between them, and thus their language has to be more explicit, particularly as far as the amount and nature of personal qualification is concerned. The importance to Bernstein's theory of codes of this context-bound versus context-free distinction cannot be overstressed, for it enables him to distinguish further between particularistic meaning and universalistic meaning.

17

The level of meaning potential is much higher in elaborated code language because of the previously noted features of less syntactic predictability and a more context-free order of meaning. But these features in turn depend to a large extent for their formulation in linguistic terms in performance upon the society of those using the different codes. The societal factors which are important in this respect are the amount and nature of the solidarity between the various members of the social class groupings, and the degree to which individuals understand the role of an individual as defined by his own particular group. Here we are at the heart of the distinction between the two language codes as expressed by Bernstein: the distinction is between the restricted code user's view of an individual as being defined and limited by his role in the group; and the elaborated code user's view of an individual as being defined and made relatively unlimited by his understanding of his own individuality.

If Bernstein's theories of linguistic codes dealt merely with the linguistic variation in the language used by various social class groups, then he would occupy a position not much different from that of, say, A. S. C. Ross who wrote on the U and Non-U distinction. But, of course, Bernstein goes farther and deeper into what he sees as the fundamental cognitive dissimilarities underlying the variations in the language codes. Bernstein has attempted with some success to explain the two codes as coming from, and making habitual by constant use, two basically different modes of thinking. The restricted code has been associated with often repeated analytic systems operating at a low level of planning. The elaborated code has been associated with a highly individual, always developing analysis characterized by long term planning. Bernstein says about the restricted code that:

'The rigid range of syntactic possibilities leads to difficulty in conveying linguistically logical sequence and stress. The verbal planning function is shortened, and this often creates in sustained speech sequences a large measure of dislocation or disjunction. The thoughts are often strung together like beads on a frame rather than following a planned sequence. A restriction in planning often creates a high degree of redundancy. This means that there may well be a great deal of repetition of information, through sequences which add little to what has already been given.'

Bernstein 1965, reprinted in Bernstein 1971, p. 134

He is convinced, as the excerpt above illustrates, that any cognitive dissimilarities that he finds in the users of the two codes are not merely differences of *style of thinking*. He argues a view, which may be described as a hard-line Whorfian view, that a language code structures modes of thinking to a very large extent. From this viewpoint, then, it is possible to explain educational failure in terms of social class and the ownership of restricted or elaborated code language.

'If a child is to succeed as he progresses through school it becomes critical for him to possess, or at least to be oriented towards, an elaborated code ...
    'Where a child is sensitive to an elaborated code the school experience for such a child is one of symbolic and social development; for a child limited to a restricted code the school experience is one of symbolic and social *change*.' (my italics)
                        Bernstein 1965, reprinted in Bernstein 1971, p. 136

On the point of the level of attainment of cognitive development, Lenneberg has some impressive evidence that a lack of language does not hinder cognitive skills:

'... grossly defective intelligence need not implicate language; nor does the *absence* of language necessarily lower cognitive skills. For instance, congenitally deaf children have in many parts of the world virtually no language or speech before they receive instruction in school. When these pre-schoolers are given non-verbal tests of concept formation they score as high as their age peers who hear.'
                                        Lenneberg 1966, p. 80

But it is more likely that Bernstein put his finger on the truly significant factor in the excerpt cited above. He suggests that a LWC child has to undergo a 'symbolic and social *change*' if he wants to succeed in school. This aspect is further discussed in relation to Labov's work later on, but it is necessary to point out here that the change involves a breaking of the psychological unity between a LWC speaker's personality and his family and local community. Schools thus contain a tendency to alienate the LWC child from his social identity and reality. Some, perhaps the majority, of LWC children are not prepared to be so alienated from their background and instead become alienated from school and from the society that prizes schooling and education.

Apocryphal Bernstein

Bernstein's position in the field of education has been central. But it has been possible, at times, to hear the name of Bernstein taken in vain. His work has been offered as a major part of the rationale behind educational planning from the nursery school to higher education. The almost religious fervour with which the work of Bernstein is associated has tended to lead to a generation of newly trained teachers with a veneration of his work hardly matched by their understanding of it. I may be accused of overstating my case in the use of the words 'almost religious fervour'. However, my own researches indicate that Bernstein's work is now firmly part of the core of orthodox ideas current in much educational and teacher trainer thinking.

Since 1969 I have been collecting the views of recently trained teachers on the state of contemporary English and the relations that the language has with its society. I chose teachers because, of course, what they think and do about language with their pupils will affect the language in the future. At the beginning I was primarily interested in the views that they held concerning attitudes to, and notions of, 'correct' English. As might be expected, their remarks on the various issues raised under 'correct' English reflected a number of differing views of a changing contemporary language. But where there was, to me, a remarkable similarity of views expressed, was in an acceptance of the idea that the working class have restricted language. This is what I call *apocryphal* Bernstein. I list below a compendium of the views of a large majority of the young teachers I interviewed. What is missing from the words on the page, though, is the amount of conviction in the way these views were expressed:

'There are WC and MC children coming from their respective backgrounds. The WC children have restricted language, the MC children do not. Children are generally proficient in one 'language' only and are thus relatively unable to switch codes.
    School uses, society requires, the MC language so that WC children who cannot change their ways of speaking do less well at school and in society. This is self-evident. WC language also involves a different (shallower?) kind of thinking thus making it even more difficult for a WC child to be successful in a mainly MC world.'

Definitely not Bernstein, you say. I agree, it's apocryphal. But similar views are commonplace. So is the remark 'These children are WC, *therefore* they have restricted language', thus implying a logical relation between the two parts of the sentence.

There are many reasons why Bernstein's work has figured so prominently in the thinking of educationalists in this country and in America. However, I want to suggest that there are two associated reasons, which have had relatively little airing, to explain the power and solidarity of Bernstein's work. I refer in the main to his apocryphal work. The first is that the bare bones of what he says, shorn of its context and its qualifications, confirms the prejudices of many teachers who are, by upbringing or education, MC. They have seen LWC children coming to school lacking in many of the things that the MC child has, such as a style of language to use in public to adults, certain social graces and so on. They have seen LWC children 'fail at school' in greater numbers than their MC peers. Apocryphal Bernstein in some ways explains why these LWC children should and do fail: the process being pre-ordained by the background and its particular effects on the language produced.

The second reason lies in his unfortunate choice of terms 'elaborate' and 'restricted' code language. Again it is worth pointing out that the qualifications that Bernstein himself makes in the use of these terms do not stay in the mind when discussing the language differences of children at school. What do stay in the mind, though, are the powerfully emotive terms. Furthermore, they carry even more powerful connotative aspects. The term 'elaborate' includes the connotations 'clever', 'intelligent', 'carefully organized'. On the other hand, the term 'restricted' has among its connotations 'limited', 'unintelligent', 'badly organized'. By the association of ideas it is only one step from deciding that a child has restricted language to deciding that he or she is 'limited, unintelligent and badly organized'. From this position it is but one step more to characterize that child in such a way for the rest of his or her school career. George Orwell called the process being 'branded on the tongue'. In this way, it is possible for a child, from the very start of his school life, to be heard as belonging either to the sheep or the goats. It is well known that a child tends to live up or down to his teacher's expectations of him: a cycle of instant judgement is created by the teacher on the grounds of language difference. This is followed by the setting of a level of expectations which is in turn followed by the partial or complete fulfilment of those expectations by the child. Apocryphal Bernstein tends to act as a catalyst in the creation and maintenance of such a cycle; a cycle, by the way, in which there is a large element of social determinism.

I have suggested that the work of Bernstein has been much misquoted and misunderstood; the ease with which he may be misunderstood may be in evidence in this essay. For this reason I turn to Halliday who appears to make one of the best summings up of the work of Bernstein. He says:

'What Bernstein's work suggests is that there may be differences in the relative orientation of different social groups towards the various functions of language in given contexts and towards the different areas of meaning that may be explored within a given function. Now if this is so, then when these differences manifest themselves in the contexts that are critical for the socialization process they may have a profound effect on the child's social learning; and therefore on his response to education, because built in to the educational process are a number of assumptions and practices that reflect differentially not only the values but also the communication patterns and learning styles of different sub-cultures. As Bernstein has pointed out, not only does this tend to favour certain modes of learning over others, but it also creates for some children a continuity of culture between home and school which it largely denies to others.'

Halliday 1973, in Bernstein 1973, pp. xiv–xv

But the measured tones of Halliday's remarks and the qualifications that Bernstein himself makes in his work do not always ring the loudest, for there exists a body of exegetical literature based upon what appears to be apocryphal Bernstein. An example of this is taken from Sugarman:

'Again, it is not just that his grammar is poor but more that he is restricted to short, descriptive, stereotyped and often incomplete sentences. He is unable to express meanings of any complexity or subtlety, to indicate how one event depends on others, results from others, precipitates others; to convey intentions, motives or feelings other than the most obvious. He cannot express these shades of meaning and in his social milieu he does not hear them expressed by others. They exist for him only in the world of school, in the world of books and those mass media that he selectively ignores.'

Sugarman 1970, pp. 245–6

It is worth noting the absolutism of 'unable to express meanings of any complexity or subtlety ... to indicate how one event depends on others ...'. The point being made here by Sugarman

22

is that the speech of the LWC is poorer in almost every respect when compared with MC speech. But in order to make this comparison much more work than exists at present needs to be done on the norms of any speech—let alone the speech of adults and children divided into social class groupings by the more or less arbitrary categories of the Registrar General. Take for instance the notion of 'incomplete utterances' mentioned by Sugarman. We just do not know what the incidence of such utterances is in 'ordinary conversation'; certainly all adult conversation contains a varying proportion of them. But can we, with any scientific accuracy, say that the language of LWC children contains a higher proportion of incomplete utterances? What about the conditions under which they occur? These are some of the questions to which no adequate answer is yet known. Until they are known, comments such as the one quoted from Sugarman must be in the realm of prejudice.

Intervention Programmes

A part of the literature of deprivation is concerned with describing what exactly is lacking from the language of the LWC child; much of the research work commissioned in Bernstein's Sociological Research Unit highlights social class differences in the maternal modes of communication, in the speech and in the socialization of children, almost always to the detriment of the LWC child or family. Another part of the literature of deprivation has made a positive attempt to change educational practice. As an example of this type of literature we turn to Bereiter and Engelmann (1966). They attempted in their book, *Teaching Disadvantaged Children in the Pre-School*, to break out from the pattern they saw existing: of language deprivation equals cognitive deprivation equals educational failure, by devising a scheme specifically for remedial language development. They describe the LWC home as providing an insufficient (for the purposes of education, anyway) linguistic and cognitive background:

'From what is known about verbal communication in lower-class homes, it would appear that the cognitive uses of language are severely restricted ... Language is primarily used to control behaviour, to express sentiments and emotions, to permit the vicarious sharing of experience and to keep the social machinery of the home running smoothly ... What is lacking ... is the use of language to explain, to describe, to instruct, to inquire, to hypothesise, to

23

analyse, to compare, to deduce, and to test. And these are the uses that are necessary for academic success.'

Bereiter and Engelmann 1966, pp. 31-2

Although the authors were concerned with what they believed to be a lower functional load carried by the language of the LWC child, their overriding preoccupation was with the structure of language, for they say:

'The speech of the severely deprived children seems to consist not of distinct words, as does the speech of middle-class children of the same age, but rather of whole phrases or sentences that function like giant words . . . these "giant word" units cannot be taken apart by the child and re-combined. . . . Instead of saying, "I ain't got no juice," he says "Uai-ga-no-ju"'.

ibid, p. 34

In order to overcome a specific lack of structures in the language of 3 and 4 year olds, they devised a programme which in many ways resembled the drills and exercises of a language laboratory. For example, an early exercise in 'identity statements' begins with 'pattern drills', and the instructions to the teacher given below illustrate what should take place in the drill:

'1. Adopt a stereotyped procedure.
   a. Present an object and give the appropriate identity statement. "This is a ball."
   b. Follow the statement with a *yes-no* question. "Is this a ball?"
   c. Answer the question. "Yes, this is a ball."
   d. Repeat the question and encourage children to answer it.
   e. Introduce *what* questions after the children have begun to respond adequately to the *yes-no* questions.'

ibid, p. 140

From then on there is a development in the complexity of the structures to be worked on, and other utterance types are dealt with. It is easy to see the reasoning behind their programmes; in order to break out of the pattern of language deprivation they thought it necessary to expand as rapidly as possible the linguistic skills of disadvantaged children *before they went to school* so that there could be a concomitant expansion in cognitive abilities.

The Bereiter and Engelmann structured language programme was seen in the mid-sixties as a reaction to some of the more traditional ways of developing children's language which had not worked too successfully. In particular their programme was seen as an antidote to unstructured attempts to give deprived children lots of vivid experience that they were supposed to lack in the inner city ghettos. Such an attempt was 'Head Start'. It was, of course, a MC response to believe that the life in the ghettos was uninteresting. There has been much criticism of the Bereiter and Engelmann approach. For example, they have been criticized for concentrating too heavily on the 'less language' hypothesis, for overemphasizing certain elements of language such as vocabulary, structure without context of speaking and labelling techniques, and for producing a programme unsuited to the learning strategies of 3 and 4 year olds. But perhaps the most enduring criticism has come only in recent years when it has been shown that the children who underwent the programme did not maintain over a two to three year period any superiority in language skills or educational attainments over their peers who did not take the programme. The experiential type of intervention programme, and now the linguistic programme, appear to have very little effect on breaking the correlation between social class and educational failure.

We have seen that a particular theory about linguistic and cognitive deprivation can become part of the social psychological background of educational thinking and planning. Rosen (1972) has suggested that Bernstein's theories have been assimilated as part of the folklore of teachers; but the theories have also become the rationale of curriculum planners and of the whole of our educational system. As an example of this it is instructive to examine the arguments of those in favour of nursery education and read a Department of Education and Science circular on the same issue (2/73 paragraph 9).

The Work of Labov

Labov has examined the language of LWC children, especially negro children, in New York. Of equal theoretical significance to the work of Bernstein, Labov's work has had nothing like the impact that Bernstein had had on the educational thinking of our time. Rosen offers a reason for the apparent power of Bernstein:

'It must be very comforting to some people to discover that the social and economic inferiority of millions is not due to anything inherently wrong with our society but to the way they talk.'

Rosen 1974, pp. 21–2

25

Labov appears to have started from a criticism of Bernstein's work concerning the relationships between the language of the MC and the LWC child. Much of the research by Bernstein and his associates tends to assume that the MC language is the norm from which the language of the LWC child deviates or does not reach. This view of a standard language has consistently led to a misunderstanding of the nature of the LWC with its own different structure and vocabulary. The notion of a 'standard language' carries with it the idea of error as well as a concentration on a value-loaded comparison rather than a description of two different systems with certain features in common.

Labov adopted a different approach from Bernstein. Working on the language of negro children he perhaps had to, because the language of these children is more different from standard English than is the case in England. He saw his task to describe and understand the system of what he called Non-Standard English *as it is*. So that he primarily described what he heard, and only then compared it with what was known about standard English. His findings have significance for the present discussion. First of all, he found that negro non-standard English had many more similarities with the standard dialect than it had differences. There were differences, but they most often related to the superficial structure of speech rather than to the underlying structure. Secondly, it was not simply the case of describing negro speech as employing fewer rules (less language) than the standard dialect. Sometimes it extended the rules of the standard dialect, sometimes, although less frequently, it contracted the rules of the standard. For examples of these: the verb 'to be' as used by the negro children was a much extended version of the standard copula verb and carried a greater meaning potential; the negro dialect did not always mark the past tense with -ed or the present tense with -s, tending rather to employ adverbials. But then I have found just this feature in the language of many children in Norwich (Rogers 1973).

Labov then devoted himself to an examination of where, why, and under what sort of conditions the non-standard dialect was used. He found, for example, that teenage negroes used their dialect to convey all the ranges of functions that the standard dialect could, but this occurred generally away from school. He also found that, again as with the standard dialect, the LWC teenager conveyed a particular set of social values in his dialect; as, separately, Adelman and Rutherford show in this collection, the use

26

of slang, the flaunting of taboo words, the style of articulation, proclaim for the teenager, membership and solidarity of a particular group. Labov's results show that in most cases his subjects were capable of repeating and handling standard English. And yet their teachers found that at school these same children and teenagers talked only a little and seemed to employ an impoverished language. In at least one sense, though, these children were quite highly sophisticated linguistically as they could switch from one code to another, *if they wanted*. An answer, perhaps, is that the children did not want to, not that they were unable to do so. The whole process of code-switching—when, how, and the constraints involved—has only been cursorily examined, and yet clearly we need to know a great deal more about it.

What Labov has done is to focus our attention onto the 'different language' hypothesis. But from his evidence gained in the field, he does not lay the blame for the apparent lack of success in schools of many LWC children onto this hypothesis. It might be thought that, by stressing the differences between the language dialects, he would naturally see these as a major contributing factor to educational failure. On the contrary, he finds little or no evidence for suggesting that the 'structural interference' or 'structural conflict', which was previously thought to exist between a negro child's dialect and the standard dialect used in school and in particular in reading books, is anything more than a relatively unimportant factor. The language differences, in his view, are not large or common enough to explain at all satisfactorily the massive illiteracy, for example, of negro children. Neither does he find any evidence for suggesting that the subjects he met were cognitively deprived. Indeed, as the title of one of his papers indicates—'The logic of non-standard English'—he has gone to great pains to illustrate the internal consistency and logicality of non-standard speech.

So if, as Labov suggests, neither the language deficit nor the language difference hypothesis is the major cause of educational failure on the part of the LWC child, we are still left with the question: what is the major cause? He argues very firmly that the LWC child finds in school not so much a language problem as an enormous problem of cultural conflict and that this conflict lies at the basis of much educational failure. It is not a case that a child cannot use language, or that the language he has hinders his reading. It is rather that he has reasons for not wanting to be seen or heard doing all those things encouraged at school. For

27

to accept the language of schooling is to accept—at least it may seem that way to other children and to the child's family—the values coded in the language of the MC. By this I do not mean aesthetic values, but rather such values as: career opportunities, studying, politics, and so on. There are also certain WC values which become under pressure at school, such as: masculinity versus effeminacy or 'cissyness', social and sexual *mores*, role of the group or street gang, job, and football crowds. The WC child is under a constant pressure to exchange his set of values for a set of MC ones while at school; the MC child is not under anything like that sort of pressure. In fact, school tends to confirm all those values the MC child finds at home. For the WC child, then, to succeed in school may well mean that he has to lose his own identity and cultural values. At this point we come back to Bernstein, who saw that this problem of change of a system of values, leading to an alienation from school, was a crucial factor in failure at school. Unlike Labov, Bernstein has not dwelt on this problem of cultural conflict arising in school, preferring to examine further the linguistic variations in different social groups. From a study of Labov's work, we are left with the fact that many LWC children see school as a place where their own culture is under attack. There remains, however, one major criticism made about Bernstein and others by Labov; that is that the sorts of interview situations used by many researchers are ones in which the LWC child does not operate very well whereas the MC child does. In Cazden's words, 'the situation is a neglected source of social class differences in language use', and has not been sufficiently considered as an independent variable. There is very clear evidence that the topic, the tasks set, and the type of questions asked, affect the amount and complexity of the language produced by the children interviewed. An example quoted by Labov illustrates the enormous effects the interview situation can have. After giving a transcript of an interview where the child is alone in a school room with a young, friendly white man, Labov goes on to say:

'The social situation which produces such defensive behaviour is that of an adult asking a lone child questions to which he obviously knows the answers, where anything the child says may well be held against him. It is, in fact, a paradigm of the school situation which prevails as reading is being taught (but not learned). We can obtain such results in our own work. ... But when we change the social situation by altering the height and power relations, introducing a close friend of the subject, and talking about things we know he is interested in, we obtain a level of excited and rapid speech.'

Labov *et al.*, 1968, Vol. 2, pp. 340–41

In England, Lawton, and, in America, Williams and Naremore, have separately found that by forcing or probing deep it is possible to reduce the effects of the school type of situation. Lawton says:

'... when the WC boys were in a situation with a friendly and sympathetic interviewer in which they were *forced* to make an abstract response or remain silent, they showed that they could communicate this kind of abstract information, although they obviously experienced some coding difficulty and were not particularly happy.'

Lawton 1970, p. 238

Another successful researcher in this field has been Rutherford who used the technique of going out of the room when recording teenagers, thus leaving the boys and girls to work out for themselves their own rules for their debate. It is a matter of regret that we are given so little language data in the published work of Bernstein and his associates that we are unable to see what sort of interview situations were used to collect the primary language data upon which the theories were built.

The Way Forward

We are left with the task of clearly listing the priorities that any educational plan must have for achieving success with the whole range of children, especially LWC children. Nothing in this paper should be taken as supporting some of the arguments of the deschoolers; on the contrary, any child going to school needs to have his language expanded—any child from any background. In particular his vocabulary relating to different registers and styles, and his ideas about appropriateness need to be enlarged so that he can offer to his communicative, cognitive and expressive faculties more and more modes of exchange. In this exchange, the currency is language. But in order to enhance the language of children, the teacher has to know where the child is now; he has to know the nature of the differences between the language of the children in his charge. Cazden has commented on this:

It is easy for us teachers to admit that we need to know more about mathematics. But because we all talk, we assume that we're all experts on language. The trouble is that the knowledge about language we require as teachers is one level beyond using it ourselves, no matter how richly we may do so. We need to know about language. And then we have to plan how to use that knowledge in the classroom.

Cazden 1972

Amongst others, Shuy (1972) has made a plea for a sense of linguistic awareness on the part of teachers to be introduced, in particular an understanding of the linguistic, social and cultural problems facing LWC children as they enter school. For it is no good merely replacing large parts of a child's linguistic competence with something else taken from the MC. This is not only wasteful and inefficient, but it is also impertinent for it implies placing a very low value on the parts or the whole that have been stripped away.

A more productive view of the social class differences in language performance is to see that, given that all varieties are capable of expressing all language functions, then there are overlapping areas of language usage where the differences are minimal. Any intervention programme should start with these overlapping areas and then adequately account for, and explain to the children, the dialectal varieties. In this way the element of 'over-kill' which has been a major source of failure of many intervention and compensatory education programmes will not be perpetrated again. This element of 'over-kill' has meant that children have been given a completely 'new' variety of language because it was felt that the 'old' one was seriously deficient. But so little that was new could be expressed that had not been possible in the 'old' language. In a short time, then, school in general, and intervention programmes in particular, were seen as simply one social group substituting its language *mores* onto another social group in a less fortunate or less powerful position in society and education.

Of course, by advocating that any language development programme should start with the culture and the language of the children whom it is designed to help, it must not be taken to imply that where clear cases of cultural impoverishment are seen to exist nothing must be done about them. Clearly not. For in such cases, not to interfere is to make the most massive interference but with a different time scheme. If it is doubted that no such programme can ever be devised, I would advise looking at the scheme in the Doughty *et al.*, *Language In Use*, as a good example of working from

30

intuitions already held by the children from whatever background. Nor must my remarks be construed as implying that, by some perversity of politics, the ownership of a restricted code is to be encouraged in a society which awards prizes on the basis of other factors. We return to Bernstein, who puts the point fairly and squarely:

'Clearly one code is not better than another; each possesses its own aesthetic, its own possibilities. Society, however, may place different values on the orders of experience elicited, maintained and progressively strengthened through the different coding systems.'

Bernstein 1965, reprinted in Bernstein 1971, p. 135

References

Bereiter, C. & Engelmann, S. (1966) *Teaching Disadvantaged Children in the Preschool*, Prentice-Hall, New Jersey.

Bernstein, B. (1965) 'A socio-linguistic approach to social learning', in Gould, J. *Penguin Survey of the Social Sciences*, London, Penguin. Reprinted in Bernstein (1971).

Bernstein, B. (1971) (ed.) *Class, Codes, and Control*, Volume 1, London, Routledge & Kegan Paul.

Bernstein, B. (1973) (ed.) *Class, Codes and Control*, Volume 2, London, Routledge & Kegan Paul.

Campbell, R. & Wales, R. (1970) 'The study of language acquisition', in Lyons, J. (ed.) *New Horizons in Linguistics*, London, Penguin.

Cazden, C. (1970) 'The neglected situation in child language research and education', *Journal of Social Issues*, 1970, 26, pp. 35–60.

Cazden, C. (1972) *Child Language and Education*, New York, Holt Rinehart & Winston.

Coulthard, M. C. (1969) 'A discussion of restricted and elaborated codes', *Educational Review*, 22, pp. 38–51.

Department of Education and Science (1973) *Nursery Education*, Circular No. 2/73, London, H.M.S.O.

Doughty, A. and P. (1974) *Using Language in Use*, London, Edward Arnold.

Doughty, P. S., Pearce, J. J., Thornton, G. M. (1971) *Language in Use*, London, Edward Arnold.

Halliday, M. A. K. (1969) 'Relevant models of language', *Educational Review*, 1969, 22, pp. 26–37. Reprinted in *Explorations in the Functions of Language*, Edward Arnold, in this series.

Halliday, M. A. K. (1973) 'Introduction' to Bernstein (ed.) 1973.

Hawkins, P. R. (1969) 'Social class, the nominal group and reference', *Language and Speech*, 12, pp. 125–35, reprinted in Bernstein (1973).

Hymes, D. (1971) 'On communicative competence', in Pride, J. B. & Holmes, J. (eds.) *Sociolinguistics*, London, Penguin, 1972.

Labov, W. (1969) *The Study of Non-Standard English*, New York, Clearinghouse for Linguistics, Center for Applied Linguistics.

Labov, W., Cohen, P., Robins, C., Lewis, J. (1968) *A Study of the Non-Standard English of Negro and Puerto Rican Speakers in New York City*, Final Report of Cooperative Research Project No. 3288, Columbia University.

Lawton, D. (1968) *Social Class, Language and Education*, London, Routledge & Kegan Paul.

Lenneberg, E. H. (ed.) (1966) *New Directions in the Study of Language*, Cambridge, Mass., M.I.T. Press.

Rogers, S. (1971) 'Language and intelligence', *Remedial Education*, 1972, 6, pp. 11–14.

Rogers, S. (1973) 'Aspects of the syntactic development of the language of children aged 5–7 years', unpublished Ph.D. thesis, University of East Anglia.

Rosen, H. (1972) *Language and Class: a critical look at the theories of Basil Bernstein*, Bristol, The Falling Wall Press.

Rosen, H. (1974) 'A social view of language in school', in *The Space Between* ..., Centre for Information on Language Teaching and Research (CILT) Report No. 10.

Shuy, R. W. (1972) 'Sociolinguistic strategies for teachers in a southern school system', paper given at 4th. AILA conference Copenhagen, August 1972, printed in *AILA Proceedings Copenhagen 1972*, Heidelberg, 1974, Julius Groos, pp. 155–71.

Sugarman, B. (1970) 'Social Class, values and behaviour in school', in Craft, M. (ed.) *Family, Class and Education*, London, Longman.

2 The language of the child culture: pattern and tradition in language acquisition and socialization

JOHN WIDDOWSON

The complex processes of cultural transmission through which children acquire language operate on many levels and in a variety of modes. The mechanics of language acquisition have been the subject of considerable research, stimulated in part by the need to understand the speech process more fully and thus to apply this knowledge for such practical ends as speech therapy and language teaching in general. Allied with these investigations is the research into the psychological aspects of language acquisition and into its sociological ramifications. The child does not merely learn the mechanics of speech production; he learns to communicate effectively in a variety of social contexts, to manipulate various codes and registers, to monitor and react to feed-back in the context of discourse, to adopt various roles during linguistic interaction, and so on.

Many of these skills are learned simply by imitation, and therefore reflect those of the immediate language group, notably the family, and particularly the mother. Some skills are learned in the context of direct teaching or demonstration, either informally through members of the immediate social group or in a more formal educational setting. Many skills, however, are learned and/ or reinforced by various traditional means operated by parents and other adults during their interaction with children, or by children interacting with each other. These traditional means of transmitting linguistic skills have received less attention than they deserve, and this is especially true of those means which not only impart or refine the motor skills of speech production and gesture, but also signal levels of meaning, social constraints and numerous cultural norms which are useful, if not essential, to adequate linguistic interaction within the culture. In moulding and developing the individual child's linguistic competence and performance, the

33

traditional verbal interchanges with adults may be concentrated, for example, on the imparting of such skills as acceptable articulation, concatenation and grammatical and syntactic structure. In addition, these interchanges communicate increasingly sophisticated information about the use of language in a social setting. Further, they convey numerous fundamental notions of familial and cultural *mores* which serve as a basis on which the child's behaviour and attitudes may be built. The work of Bernstein,[1] and more recently of Cook-Gumperz,[2] has drawn attention to the importance of these linguistic forms, although the purely traditional nature of such usages is not the main thrust of their enquiries.

I should like to explore here some of the traditional means whereby basic linguistic skills are communicated, particularly at the family level, and, more particularly, how these familial and cultural traditions play a part in moulding, or even conditioning, certain aspects of the child's behaviour and attitudes, at least in his early years. The number and the importance of such traditional verbal usages, of course, varies from culture to culture and from group to group. They are apparently used with greater frequency and impact in those families and social groups which have inherited and maintain an extensive and varied set of homogeneous traditions. Adult/child relationships, and therefore also their verbal interaction, may well differ, for example, in a close-knit working-class family as distinct from, say, a middle- or upper-class family in West-European urban society. Notwithstanding Bernstein's findings about the differences between such verbal interaction in working-class and middle-class British families,[3] it is clear, however, that neither class is exclusively person-oriented or position-oriented in its verbal interaction with children in the context of social control. This is obvious, for example, in upper-class and middle-class families in which the day-to-day care of the child may be the responsibility of a nurse or other person not a member of the family and whose background and traditions may differ radically from those of the parents. In such families the mother herself may be in close contact with the child comparatively rarely, and thus interact with him only minimally on the linguistic level. Consequently, the nurse's controlling of his behaviour may be primarily position-oriented, while the less frequent contact with the mother in the context of social control may be more person-oriented.

As might be expected, the traditional learning systems are often more extensive, deeper and more tenacious in the lower levels of

34

British society than in the upper, where more formal learning systems tend to predominate and verbal social controls are more likely to be person-oriented. Social learning and socialization, according to Bernstein, operate through sociolinguistic codes. By means of these codes a child learns which behavioural options are open to him and he is able to choose which option to take within the coding system, whether it be 'restricted' or 'elaborated'. Bernstein's research has indicated that the restricted code is more typical of lower-class families and that the elaborated code is more typical of middle-class families.[4] Even if it were possible to draw a clearcut division between these two classes, one might question whether this generalization is universally valid. It would be interesting to investigate, for instance, how the codes are used, especially in actual day-by-day contexts of social control, in families of indefinite or 'mixed' social class in which one parent, for example, may tend to use the restricted code and the other the elaborated code when offering verbal behavioural guidelines to children.

The recognition, use and effectiveness of these codes, however, depends, at least in part, on a shared corpus of traditional linguistic and paralinguistic expression, particularly at the family level. Certain sounds, gestures, words, phrases and other usages such as proverbs and rhymes constitute an important part of the traditional patterns of verbal interaction within individual families. Such usages in turn reflect and are reflected by parallel forms and attitudes in the wider surrounding culture. They form part of a complex pattern of traditions which include customs and beliefs about pregnancy, birth, child-rearing and children, for example, expressed in many traditional verbal forms. As language is itself central to a given cultural tradition, and it is through language that the *mores* of the group are transmitted, it follows that the patterning of traditional oral usages in the child's formative years plays a crucial role in his socialization. Some of the usages are communicated by adults to each other, but most are used specifically in the context of interaction between adult and child.

The aim of this brief study is to trace some of the traditional verbal usages employed by English adults of lower- and middle-class backgrounds during their interaction with children, especially in the context of language acquisition, socialization and social control. The study stems from my fieldwork and research, mainly in Yorkshire and neighbouring countries of northern England, concentrating attention on a specific lower-middle-class family originating from the Sheffield area. This family is characterized by a considerable degree of social mobility from working class to middle class during the past fifty years. Within this family group, position-oriented controls predominate, but person-oriented controls have increased as the family has moved away from its original socio-economic status. The family has also moved from place to place, the trend being from an urban to a semi-rural environment. While such a family may be in some ways unusual, it preserves a remarkably homogeneous set of traditions. Preliminary investigation indicates that many of these traditions are shared by other families, not only in Yorkshire but elsewhere in northern England and beyond.

A major problem in presenting data on traditional verbal usages addressed to children is that the material itself is difficult to set down in written form, especially without recourse to full contextual description and phonetic transcription. As might be expected, many of the expressions used are often amusingly facile, particularly when written. This is especially true of baby talk, a genre with which we are all familiar yet which remains little investigated, perhaps because of the problems outlined here. Nevertheless, these simple day-to-day utterances are an important means whereby the young child not only acquires receptive and expressive linguistic skills but also the predictability essential to the process of socialization. A data-oriented approach to such material has the advantage of immediacy in reminding us of everyday usages with which we are familiar, but which have escaped our critical attention.

This study also draws on the resources of the Archives of Cultural Tradition at the University of Sheffield where a preliminary research project investigating traditional verbal social controls was initiated through the Survey of Language and Folklore in 1971. This ongoing project continues to yield extensive information on traditional verbal usage from all parts of the British Isles, and indicates the broad trends of such traditions as well as their regional and socio-economic patterning and variation. Its primary focus is the identification and analysis of traditional verbal patterns used repeatedly in appropriate contexts to socialize a child, or as Birdwhistell puts it, to establish predictability of the child's behaviour.[5]

Even before a child is born, the parents and other adults in the kinship group, together with their friends and neighbours, prepare for the new arrival in certain traditional ways. Some aspects of these traditional preparations give rise to various expressions

36

which differ from group to group. Aside from the patterned phrases concerning prediction of the infant's sex—whether, for example, the mother is said to be 'big in the back' or 'carrying the baby high (or low)' during pregnancy—the unborn child is spoken of as if it were already a member of the family. Parents and other adults refer to it as 'he' or 'she', or perhaps give it a name or pet name when referring to it in conversation. When the child moves in the womb, this activity often becomes the focus of semi-euphemistic conversation between wife and husband during which the husband may be initiated into the regrouping of familial patterns which the expected child will bring about by its presence. The mother, especially in middle-class families, may also prepare other children in the family for the baby's arrival by encouraging them on occasion to feel the unborn baby moving and by explaining, often in traditional terms, how the infant is growing 'in Mummy's tummy'. The semi-euphemistic use of 'tummy' is typical of such references and explanations by parents when speaking to children, and illustrates the link between baby talk and euphemism in such contexts. Between themselves, on the other hand, parents may talk about the pregnancy at a completely different linguistic and semantic level, commenting on or joking about the physiological changes involved, and particularly the difficulties of the final weeks of pregnancy. During this final stage the verbal interaction between the parents is especially important in their readjustment of roles, and speculation about the sex of the child also plays a part in initiating these verbal exchanges. In the family from the Sheffield area which forms one focus of this study, one grandmother always says of such speculations, 'I don't mind whether it's a boy or a girl as long as it's all right,' and similar expressions which emphasize the view that the first essential is the child's (and the mother's) health rather than the sex of the child. This attitude runs counter to the common belief among English people, and indeed in most other cultures, that the preferred first-born is a boy. The need for a first-born son to carry on the inheritance and to help and succeed the father in his occupation or profession has long been in decline in western urban tradition, yet there is still some obligation to make excuses for the first-born girl by saying, for example, that it is lucky for a girl to be born first. The repetition in such contexts of statements to this effect is one means by which society compensates parents whose first-born is a girl. Such statements also have similar semantic and structural patterning. If the child is inactive during the

37

final weeks before birth, or if it is overdue, Yorkshire people say it will be 'a lazy boy' or 'a dozy lad'—commenting in semi-humorous terms on the supposed characteristics of the child and of boys in general. Sometimes the predictions involve linguistic ambiguity, often at the dialectal level, as in the South Yorkshire belief that heartburn suffered by the mother during pregnancy will cause the child to have 'lots of 'air (i.e. hair)'.

In sharp contrast with these mainly integrative usages within the family group, traditional references to pregnancy outside the group, especially among young men, are often risqué or ribald. Pregnancy, especially unwanted pregnancy, is referred to by a surprisingly large number of slang and dialectal expressions. These include: 'She's in the club', 'She's got a bun in the oven', 'She's podding', 'She's got one up the spout', and numerous similar uncomplimentary euphemisms, which draw attention to the changed status of the mother. On the other hand, traditional comments from within the family group and from outside observers well-disposed to the mother, may refer to the common folk belief that pregnancy enhances a woman's health and beauty. Typical of traditional ways of expressing this belief is the statement about a young mother which I tape-recorded during an interview with a retired East Yorkshire fisherman in 1960: 'She never looks no better bar when she's carryin'.' There is ample corroboration in other parts of England for both the belief and its formulaic expression. Even though a pregnant woman may appear more beautiful, however, traditional, essentially Victorian, attitudes still occasionally persist, especially among older middle-class women, regarding the acceptability of a woman being seen in a public place during the advanced stage of pregnancy. Radical changes in such attitudes have taken place in the past thirty years, yet one grandmother in the Sheffield family still invariably uses the word 'brazen', with strong pejorative connotations, when referring to such a woman, and her comments and intonation indicate her scorn of such behaviour, and stigmatize it as socially unacceptable, notwithstanding the advent of stylish maternity wear and the other reasons advanced by younger members of the family in defence of their dissenting opinions. The repetition of such expressions within the family group might be expected to mould certain behavioural responses. These, however, are by no means limited to simple acquiescence. On the contrary, in this particular family, the repeated verbal references sometimes serve to emphasize the generation gap and are a source of dissonance through

38

which younger members of the family develop attitudes and behavioural patterns at variance with those of their elder familial mentors. Nevertheless, at the etic† level each individual expression of such familial attitudes and *mores* establishes or reinforces certain normative guidelines within which the younger members of the family are encouraged to adopt predictable patterns of behaviour which coincide with or approximate to those of the elder members who constitute the leaders or the control group in a child's early years. The repetition of certain words, phrases, proverbs and other expressions in similar contexts over a period of time establishes a set of linguistic controls at the emic level. While the exact wording may vary with each etic realization, the group is aware of the emic notion underlying each etic utterance. It is immaterial whether grandmother says, for example, 'That brazen hussy is out walking in *that* condition,' or 'Fancy anyone walking out looking like *that*—the brazen hussy'. Through these transformations the emic notion, 'A woman who goes out while heavily pregnant is shameless,' is communicated and its repetition is an affirmation of attitude on the part of the speaker—a challenge to other members of the group to accept (and it is intended that they should) or reject.

It is into this complex of patterned behaviour and expression that the child is born. Among all the other aspects of linguistic and social codes which he has to learn, he has to recognize, respond to and learn to use these many expressions of the familial *mores* which surround him from the beginning. They in turn reflect the *mores* of the wider surrounding culture. As Birdwhistell puts it: 'The child is born into a society already keyed for his coming. A system exists into which he must be assimilated if the society is to sustain itself.'⁶ At the level of the family it is the mother who is primarily responsible for the socialization of the very young child. It is primarily her language, her attitudes and her *mores* which he assimilates in these formative years, and much information is imparted by traditional means, communicated in traditional forms, consciously or otherwise. Mothers and other women speculating about an expected child already express their protective attitude in a number of ways. Among these, one of the more obvious is the reiteration of such adjectives as 'little' whenever they refer to the child. They say, for example, 'I wonder if

† The terms etic and emic are taken from phonetic and phonemic. Etic is a general term referring to all possible data; emic refers to the way in which the data bears upon a particular case.

it will be a little boy or a little girl,' emphasizing the obvious small-ness of a newborn infant as if this was somehow unexpected and required that attention be drawn to it. The constant use of this adjective serves to remind the group of the infant's smallness and vulnerability and thus nurtures protective attitudes towards him. This form of linguistic usage continues, though with decreasing frequency, for a considerable time after the child is born. Older, usually female, relatives ask others to 'Look at his/her lovely little hands/fingers/feet/toes,' for example, and specifically praise their smallness. Examples of such usages are numerous: 'Isn't she a lovely little thing!'; 'You're a nice little boy, aren't you?'; and so on. The semantic range of the adjective 'little' changes radically as the child grows older and shifts from a purely protective func-tion to one in which social control is incipient or overt. A child of, say, six or seven may be referred to as 'A little nuisance/terror/horror,' either seriously or humorously, and in such contexts the adjective serves not to indicate the adult's protective or affec-tionate role, but to emphasize the child's non-adult status and even imply that he may continue to display such undesirable char-acteristics in the future. At quite an early stage of infancy mothers and other adults may counter the protectiveness of such words as 'little' and instead praise the child's size or growth: 'What a big boy you are'; 'You're growing into such a big boy now', in-stilling, as it were, a sense of the child's potential physical growth on the one hand, while assuring him of protection on the other.

The newborn infant enters a context of communication at birth. He utters his first cries in reflex response to the stimulus of physical action immediately after birth and his cries help to initiate the process of breathing. From that time on, during the first few months of infancy his cries will signal to others that he needs atten-tion. The mother relies on this basic two-signal communication system in which crying signals the need for attention, and the absence of crying normally means that the infant is comfortable or asleep. Although his crying and other vocalization are mainly the result of reflexes in the first two months of life, he soon learns that he can gain attention through crying and may therefore extend the range of communication by the eventual realization that his cries are responded to in contexts other than those of physi-cal comfort and discomfort. The development of receptive skills after the first two months is indicated by his ability to distinguish the human voice from other sounds, and his response to that voice. Even before this, however, the socialization process has begun.

In the earliest stages it is largely tactile—holding, cuddling or caressing the infant, for example—but from the earliest stages it includes a considerable degree of gestural and verbal communication. Mothers, other adults and also older children use smiles and more exaggerated facial expressions such as raising their eyebrows, opening their eyes wide and puckering their lips as if to say 'Ooh!', while jutting the face out towards the child. All these encourage the child to respond and their repetition leads to his realization of a sense of protection and well-being.

A common communicative device used in the Sheffield family, which I have also observed frequently elsewhere in northern England, is the use of three or more clicking sounds, pronounced with the tip of the tongue against the upper teeth and the blade of the tongue against the alveolar ridge. This sound, usually rendered in print as 'tut tut,' has a totally different meaning in the context of adult communication, where it signals disapproval, and it can also be used in this way when adults speak to children. When addressed in a friendly way to very young children, however, the sound is repeated quickly, usually three, four, five or six 'clicks'. It is said with spread or neutral lips which form part of a smile, and the head is tilted slightly back, the eyebrows raised and the eyes opened unusually wide. Sometimes the clicks are pronounced as the head is shaken slowly from side to side, and the face again adopts an exaggerated smiling posture. As the child's receptive skills develop he begins to respond to these gestures and sounds, often by smiling himself. The smile is encouraged by other tactile devices. One of these is gently to pinch the child's cheeks between the thumb and forefinger. Another is to hold the child's chin between the thumb and forefinger so that the chin rests between them and move his head gently from side to side. Both of these actions may cause the child to smile, and the first seems to depend partly on reflex action in that the slight pressure on the cheeks often causes his mouth to form a smile. By smiling himself, or by saying 'That's a nice smile', 'What a lovely little smile', and so on, the adult apparently reinforces his encouragement of the child's smile, and himself provides a model for the child to imitate. Gestural communication of this kind is found, in the Sheffield family, for example, at a very early stage of the child's development. These gestures are passed on in familial and local tradition and form an important part of the communication process.

When the child's receptive skills are still undeveloped, mothers, and especially older female relatives, address a great deal of verbal communication to him, which, certainly in the initial stages, he is unable to comprehend. The effect of such speech acts, however, is to initiate the child into certain basic contexts of communication. By way of illustration I should like to describe briefly two such kinds of verbalizing observed in the Sheffield family. The first occurred in the context of bottle-feeding the baby. At quite an early stage the baby responds to food with excited movements and sounds. Before feeding him, the mother mimed the feeding process, pretending to drink from the bottle and saying, 'Nice. Nice milkies. Ooh, it does taste good [dɒd].' The same kind of verbalizing was also evident when the baby was encouraged to drink the last few drops of milk. At the end of every feeding session the mother held up the empty bottle, shook it as if to show it was empty, and said, 'All gone!' once or twice. She then went through the ritual of bringing up the child's wind, patting him gently on the back while he was sitting upright or putting him over her shoulder and patting his back. When the child finally burped she responded with, 'That's a good boy', 'That's a clever boy' and similar phrases. From the age of about four months, however, she would more often say 'Excuse me', 'Pardon me' or 'I beg your pardon' after the child burped, made a 'raspberry' noise, etc. The grandmother invariably responded to such noises by saying, 'I beg your pardon and grant you grace.' Each of these sets of responses by the mother marks a stage in the social development of the child. At a later stage he learns that belching is not encouraged in certain social situations and apologizes for any lapses by means of the linguistic formulas repeatedly spoken by the mother, by proxy, as it were, during these situations.

A second kind of incident is one in which the child is told a story or given an account of events before his receptive skills have developed. Here again the child is initiated into a context of communication in which both the linguistic forms and concepts have little, if any, meaning for him. Even so, in listening repeatedly to such verbalizing in similar contexts he is given the opportunity to develop receptive skills by learning and by imitation. During these incidents the child sits on the adult's knee or in the arms and has the reassurance of being held. A typical verbal sequence in the Sheffield family goes as follows:

'²It's ă lŏvelў sûnnў ⁴dáy ³oŭtsíde⁴. ⁻ ⁴M⁻r. Sún iš

shíniṅg²⁻²aṅd áll thĕ ³bírds aře ⁴síngiṅg. ⁻⁴Loók!³⁻³Thĕre's ă

bîg ⁴bús gôiňg pâst.²⁻⁴Whát ǎ ²bîg bûs!²⁻² İ wóndĕr whère iťs
³góiňg². ↘ ²Pĕrhâps iťs gôiňg ǎ lóng lóng wây. ↘ ʼ⁷

Of course, virtually any quotation from such adult verbalizing
addressed to very young infants exhibits variation according to
context, personality and so on. Nevertheless, such speech is
marked by certain distinctive characteristics. The intonation, for
example, is characterized by exaggerated changes of pitch and
the 'sing-song' tune typical of much adult speech addressed to very
young children. In particular, terminals tend to be sustained
rather than falling. Strongest and secondary stresses, and high
pitches predominate. Although the vocabulary is simple, this passage is remarkably free of 'baby talk', although in other observed
incidents reduplicative forms and diminutives were more frequently used. All the sentences are short and simple or occasionally compound. Rhetorical devices such as the personification of
the sun and the frequent use of attention-getting exclamations
play a part in encouraging the child's response. Such expressions
are part of the stock of familial and cultural usages traditionally
employed in the socializing of children. The forms are often
learned within the family group, especially by daughters learning
from their mothers, as they also learn much about the day-to-day
care of the child.

The impact of such verbalizing upon the development of the
child's receptive skills is difficult if not impossible to gauge. It
seems probable, however, that it plays a part in developing these
skills, and perhaps also, to a lesser extent, in developing his expressive competence. The expressive skills, however, also rely in
their development on certain traditional methods of expression.
During the babbling stage, for example, which normally begins
in about the third month, parents may seize upon certain babbled
sounds which coincidentally sound like words, and by repeating
them when speaking to the child, often in conjunction with the
referent, e.g. book, mummy, etc., they encourage the child to pronounce these sounds again and thus gradually develop an association of sound with referent. This is done, for example, by holding
up a book for the child to see and repeatedly saying the word book,
or pointing to the mother and repeating the word mummy.

Children acquire expressive competence by a combined process
of reduplication and echoic response. Each of these methods of
acquisition is often initiated and reinforced by traditional usages.
Baby talk used by adults in speaking to children, for example,

43

includes many reduplicative forms. Of these, forms such as babba, mamma and bye-bye have the additional virtue that the bilabial consonants are 'visible' and therefore perhaps easier to imitate. The impact of this 'visibility' is increased by the many traditional modes of communicative behaviour in which the face, especially the protruding lips, is jutted towards the child in various games and other forms of social and linguistic interaction. This helps to concentrate attention on the mouth which, through feeding and other means, is the first part of the body to be socialized. In the reduplicative phase of developing expressive skills the child repeats the syllables many times, or sometimes pronounces only one syllable. Constant repetition of the disyllabic form by the adults helps him to refine his echoic response. Sometimes a monosyllabic form used in baby talk may exist alongside a disyllabic form with a different meaning. For example, in South Yorkshire children are taught to say 'ta' (thank you) as early as three or four months. If the child is given something or reaches out for something, the word 'ta' is said as the object is proffered. A little later when the child learns to say 'ta', the object may be gently withheld until he says the word. This is one of several words in baby talk which also persist in informal usage at the adult level. In the Sheffield area this is seen, for instance, in the widespread use of the phrase 'Ta, love', especially by working-class and lower-middle-class adults in informal contexts. When reduplicated, however, the syllable ta has a totally different set of meanings. In the Sheffield family the word tata was among the earliest taught to the children. It has two basic senses: 'goodbye' and 'walk' (ride in pram, car, bus, train, etc.). When used to mean 'goodbye' the word is taught by frequent repetition in the situational context of departure, and a distinctive wave of the hand is used to accompany the word. Sometimes the mother or other adult takes hold of the child's arm and moves it in response to the wave so that the child is taught both the word and the gesture simultaneously.[8] In my experience the child learns the gesture before he learns the word, but he learns to associate the two. The second meaning of the word is often taught as the child is being dressed to go out. Adults say, 'Is Billy going for a tata?', 'Would he like to go for a little tata?' and so on. Notice here, as in so much of the speech addressed to children, the third person form of address is used. The two meanings of tata are related semantically through the notion of departure, and this inter-relationship is reinforced by the exchange of tatas and waves when the child is about to go

44

outdoors for a walk. The reduplicative form bye-bye is also used in place of tata in the sense of 'goodbye', but when used with a final -s- in the second syllable has the meaning of 'sleep'—'Time for bye-byes', 'Time you went to bye-byes,' etc. In the Sheffield family, the forms biddy-byes, and biddy-bumps or biddy bum-petties were also used by the grandmother, the latter two perhaps being her own inventions.[9] The inventory of reduplicative terms in this family is extensive. It includes, for example, brek-brek (breakfast); bun-bun (rabbit); bye-bye (goodbye); bye-byes (sleep); choc-choc (chocolate); chuck-chuck (hen); din-din(s) (dinner); eye-pyes (eyes); gee-gee (horse); pap-pap (car); pim-pim (finger—apparently an imitation of one's child attempt to pronounce finger); pud-pud (pudding); puff-puff (train); quack-quack (duck); sup-sup(s) (supper); tata (goodbye, walk); tick-tick (watch); wee-wee (urine, urination); woof-woof (dog); yooey-yooeys, yooey-yooey-yooeys [juɪ juːz] [juɪ juɪ juːz] (rubber gloves—individual child's onomatopoeic imitation of squeaking sound made by the gloves; term confined to the five members of the immediate family sub-group). A further semantic dimension and echoic potential is found in such reduplicative forms which not only encourage imitation by duplication of the sound pattern but also echo the sound made by the creature or object concerned. This clearly helps the child to associate the word with its referent or at least to learn the sound made by the referent. Children evidently have no difficulty in acquiring the adult words at an early or later stage. This was brought home vividly to me when one of the children in the Sheffield family said his first word—[gɔk] (duck) at the age of ten months, even though the form quack-quack was frequently used when speaking to him. The use of re-duplicatives has the virtue of encouraging the child to practise pronunciation of similar sounds, gaining confidence as he does so. At the same time he begins to associate words with their referents and to learn something of the onomatopoeic, metaphorical and rhyming characteristics of language. The persistence of such forms as bye-bye in informal adult usage also suggests that such words act as useful alternatives to more formal usages in certain contexts.

A number of words in baby talk have the dual function of nam-ing the referent and also suggesting the sound it makes or some quality about it. Thus moo-cow, chucky-hen/chucky-fowl are not reduplicative but combine an echo of the sound the animal makes with the normal adult name. Such words constitute an intermedi-ate stage between simple reduplication and the adult form. Their semantic range is also greater, as, for example, in chucky-egg where the first element draws on forms such as chuck-chuck and chucky-hen to suggest the origin of the egg. In this way such words are linked through the semantic reference suggested by the echoic element which itself is readily assimilated by the child. One might add here that as we move further and further away from a land-based economy, the relevance of such references, and therefore the use of forms based on them, must decline. The field research indicates a considerable decline of baby talk, for these, and also for many other reasons. Nevertheless, urban as well as rural families in northern England continue to use such forms, and the Sheffield family, stemming from urban tradition but living mostly in semi-rural or rural areas, uses a number of these terms, including, for example: checky-pig (pig—also piggy-jack); chucky-egg (egg); chucky-hen/fowl (hen); moo-cow (cow); puffer-train. Forms such as chucky-hen, checky-pig, etc., and especially their reduplicative equivalents such as chick-chick, chuck-chuck, check-check, etc., when used in rural contexts, have the additional dimension that they are composed wholly or partially of forms used to call animals. In the Sheffield family, for example, young chickens are called by the word chick, usually five times in quick succession. To call hens the word chuck is used in a similar way, and check is used to call pigs.

More extensive, however, is the Sheffield family's use of baby talk words which are neither reduplicative nor necessarily echoic. They fall into six reference groups central to the child's environment:

1. Parts of the body and bodily functions, etc., e.g.: big tries (defecation, faeces); billy wind(s), billy windums (cholic); bogey (nasal mucus); dannies (hands); little man (penis); niddy, niddy nose (nose); peeky (penis—apparently invented by one of the children and adopted by younger members of the family); peepies (eyes); peggies (teeth); sleepy man (deposit in corner of eyes); tussies, tussy-pegs (teeth); woodler ['wuːdlə] (penis).
2. Food, drink and meals, e.g.: bicky (biscuit); brecky (breakfast); dinky, dinkies (drink).
3. Clothing, e.g.: pods, poddies, shoe pods (shoes).
4. Kinship, e.g.: dad-dad, later daddy (father); ['gandad][10] (grandfather—used with and by children in the youngest section of the family in the last nine years); ['glɔmpɑː]

46

(grandpa—early mispronunciation by one child, adopted by older family members); mum-mum, later mummy (mother); nanny, later grannie (grandmother).
5. Animals, e.g.: bunny, bunny rabbit (rabbit); dicky bird (bird); pussy, pussycat (cat).
6. Objects in the child's immediate environment, e.g.: akumba [a'ʔɔmba] (spectacle case; onomatopoeic imitation by very young child of sound of spectacle case closing; adopted by members of family in the form [a'kɔmba]); ding ding, dinger, ding dong (bell); mutty (dummy teat; word used only by one grandmother. All other members use dummy); old pipe (dummy teat; used in the context of discouraging the child from needing the teat); tick tock (clock).

Some of these forms are in general use, others are especially common among lower and lower middle-class families elsewhere, some are dialectal and some (e.g. woodler, big tries) may be inventions confined to the family. They display a number of basic characteristics:

1. The use of diminutive endings. These are added to any word in the context of speaking to children and constitute the most distinctive feature of baby talk. Thus the lexical inventory of baby talk may be infinitely extended by the addition of -y or -ie to any existing word, e.g. footy, potty, handy, housy, doggy, etc. This suffix also typifies kinship terms and many other words used in informal and intimate styles.
2. A playful or humorous attempt to make things sound more familiar, often by using a familiar name, e.g. billy wind, dicky bird, etc.
3. Euphemism. This is commonly used with reference to certain parts of the body and to bodily functions which must be referred to in the context of washing, toilet training and the like. Whereas in the Sheffield family the euphemism big tries was replaced at a later stage by business ('Go and do your business'), the trend of many parents, certainly in the middle class, nowadays is to refer to the parts of the body in a more 'direct' way, although, interestingly enough, we use Latin terms, for example, in such references, and this is a kind of euphemism in itself.

It is interesting to note that two picturesque forms commonly known in South Yorkshire are not used in the baby talk of the

47

Sheffield family. These words are poppo or bobbo (horse) and lillilow ['lɪlɪlou] (a glimmering light). Gee-gee was substituted for the first concept, and no special word was used instead of the second. Both forms are dialectal, poppo and bobbo being apparently localized to South Yorkshire and North Derbyshire, and when I asked a great-aunt in the family why these were not used, she replied, with some dignity, 'Oh, we don't use words like that in *our* family,'[11] implying that they were lower-class usages. The same reaction came from one of the grandmothers when she was asked about the word babba (faeces) used by a Derbyshire woman who came to help in the house. The word was never used by members of the family, though remembered by one of the sons who recalled his mother's strong negative reaction to its use. From evidence of this kind there is a demonstrable relationship between such usages and socio-economic class. Even more obvious is the decline of such usages, especially in middle-class but also in lower-class families, in England in recent years, influenced partly by the change of family structure from nuclear to extended, and partly by new theories and methods of child-rearing which are often unsympathetic to the traditional modes of informal instruction within the family. Despite its declining use, baby talk may help to encourage communication, to provide pronunciation practice and examples of rhyme and rhythm through reduplicative forms and to suggest the existence of different semantic levels and degrees of linguistic acceptability. Baby talk functions as an informal teaching device which may improve both the receptive and expressive linguistic skills of the child and help in his socialization at the same time.

The acquisition of expressive skills is also assisted by patterned informal teaching within the family group. Adults provide imitative models for the child in order to encourage his communication, to establish and refine basic articulation patterns, and at a later stage to establish and refine his phonological, morphological, grammatical and syntactical competence and to develop his lexical inventory. At its most rudimentary this informal teaching involves engaging the child in a simple language game in which the adult, for example, repeats one or more of the random sounds uttered by the child during the babbling stage. An uncle in the Sheffield family was observed to lean over the pram in which a child of some three months was lying and to repeat the syllable [ba] several times, with several seconds pause between each utterance. As he did so, the same paralinguistic features—slow, deliberate articulation, raised eyebrows, eyes opened unusually wide, head thrust forward—noted as the typical communicative behaviour in such contexts, were clearly in evidence. These unusual and exaggerated facial expressions help to catch the child's attention and he comes to recognize that they connote an element of play to which he responds, first with a smile, later by imitation of the sounds, and even sometimes of the facial expressions. Games of this kind help to bridge the gap between the preverbal child's unsystematic babbling and his ability to consciously select and pronounce a given sound at will.

Attempts are also made to correct faulty articulation by providing an imitative model. Adults will pronounce the sound as they know it, and repeat it to encourage imitation. For a time they may adopt the child's misencoding—as was the case with the word [gɒk] (duck) in the Sheffield family—before attempting to refine the pronunciation. In this case the repetition of [dɒk] by the adults when speaking to the child resulted in the desired refinement, but it is interesting to note that the northern dialectal [ɒ] was not refined to [ʌ] until the child attended pre-school playgroup at the age of four and imitated models of pronunciation from outside the family group. The problems of acquiring expressive skills in the dialect of the family, and the conflicts which arise later when the child comes into contact with another dialect system, are too complex to deal with here, but they obviously merit further study.

The formulaic characteristics of such informal corrective teaching within the family are well known. Adults say, for instance, 'Not [gɒk] [dɒk]', 'It's not [gə] it's [bə]',[12] 'Don't say [gɒk], say [dɒk]', 'We don't say [gɒk], we say [dɒk]', etc. This latter formula is of course also commonly used to communicate familial and cultural behavioural norms which the child is encouraged to adopt. Hence the frequency of such traditional formulas as 'We don't say things like that, do we?', 'Nice little girls don't do that', 'That's not the way we behave at the table, is it?', 'Only naughty boys do that', etc. The similar patterning of such utterances provides a contextual continuity recognizable to the child, as do the few typical linguistic patterns used in threats and other more overt means of verbal social control.

In addition to the context of informal teaching of language skills, the receptive competence of the child may be extended by traditional explanations of strange and often frightening things present in the environment. If a very young child is frightened

49

by a sudden loud noise or unexpected movement, for example, he is soothed by being picked up and cuddled. Certain typical verbal patterns are used during this period of reassurance. The person, animal, machine, etc. which startled or frightened the child is censured by the adult with such words as 'Did that naughty old dog frighten you when he barked, then? Oh, it's a shame! Never mind! It's gone now.' These reassuring words (1) explain the origin of the offending sound; (2) censure the originator of it; (3) sympathize with the child's feelings; (4) reassure him that the frightening situation is over. At the same time the adult affirms his own role as the child's protector, as he does also when using threats to control the child's behaviour in other situations.

More elaborate means are traditionally used to explain various natural phenomena to the young child. These explanations usually take the form of dites or recurrent substantive motifs, as Hand designates them,[13] which are found widely distributed throughout Europe and North America, although they are apparently in decline in England. The dites display a remarkable similarity of form and content in various cultures and are used to account for various natural phenomena. One particularly interesting and persistent set of such dites is used to refer to four common phenomena: snow, thunder, rain and sunshine occurring simultaneously, and the configuration of the moon. They serve the dual purpose of satisfying the young child's curiosity about or allaying his fears of these phenomena and also help to arouse his awareness of different semantic levels by their metaphorical nature. In addition, they suggest, or are accompanied by, an aetiological legend which may expand the brief spoken explanation into a story. Such stories, of course, become familiar to the child as he is introduced to folktales and legends, either from oral tradition, or by having them read aloud. Their patterned structure may add a further dimension to his receptive competence, and the morality implicit in many folktales may also have a bearing on his socialization.[14] When a small child first sees snow falling, the traditional explanations in England usually refer to feathers or the plucking of geese, e.g. 'The old woman is plucking her geese.' In South Yorkshire this motif is echoed in the children's rhyme:

> Ally ally aster
> Snow snow faster,
> Pluckin' geese in Scotland
> An' sendin' feathers 'ere.

In the same region when thunder is heard, the child's fears are allayed by references such as 'T'owd lad's rollin' barrels upstairs,' or in Lincolnshire, 'Elephants are dancing.' A modern semi-scientific version is that thunder is caused by 'clouds bumping together'. On the other hand, thunder is still a cause of fear, even among adults, and may be referred to in threats used to encourage good behaviour. In such threats thunder is often represented as the angry voice of God.

When rain falls while the sun is shining, a common saying is 'It's only a sunshower; it won't wet you,' but older people remember the once widespread saying 'The Devil is beating his wife' with reference to this phenomenon.[15] Traditional explanations about the configuration of the moon include references to the man in the moon, whose features are pointed out, or who is shown to have a bundle of wood on his back and to be accompanied by a dog. Children are also told why he was put there—often for gathering wood on a Sunday—and in this way the aetiological legend includes an implied moral about the observance of Sunday. It is difficult to gauge the impact which such sayings and legends have on the young child, but it is reasonable to suppose that they increase his receptive competence by introducing him to metaphor and to a poetic rather than a scientific explanation of the phenomena at an age when scientific explanation is difficult, if not impossible. At another level, the sayings allay the child's fears and may also include some reference to morality, whether stated or implied.

Proverbs and proverbial sayings form another genre of traditional usage employed in the context of social control. Insofar as such usages encapsulate certain aspects of the familial and cultural *mores*, they clearly have an important part to play in the socialization of the child. Their brevity, pithiness, structural patterning (including balance, antithesis, alliteration and assonance), word play and metaphorical form, reinforced by frequent repetition in similar contexts, present the child with opportunities to extend his receptive competence, and also, through imitation, to improve his expressive competence and performance. At the same time they communicate, in memorable form, information highly relevant to the socialization of the child. A few examples used in the Sheffield family will illustrate the range and potential of such usages. The notion, for instance, that waste is a sin, handed down from Victorian times and reinforced by the privations of the Depression and the two World Wars, is constantly reiterated in the proverbial saying, 'Waste not, want not.' This was used with trenchant effect apropos of children wasting food, for example. The grandfather in the Sheffield family deprecates greediness by saying, 'You should eat to live, lad, not live to eat.' A similar notion is that good plain food is best for a child, so when he asks for sauce or pickles he is told, 'Hunger is the best sauce.' The saying need not be proverbial. If a child fails to eat all that is set before him, he is told to clean up his plate, with the constant adjuration, 'Don't leave a saucy plate.' A child trying to do something too hurriedly evokes the proverb, 'More haste, less speed'; if he is staring vacantly with his mouth open he is asked, 'Are you catching flies?', and when he chatters inconsequentially, he is told sternly and scornfully that, 'An empty cart makes the most rattle.' Even from such a brief sampling of the material it is clear that such usages continue to fulfil several functions in developing the child's linguistic competence and increasing the predictability of his behaviour.

The exercising of verbal social control of children by adults inevitably produces considerable tension between them. Direct confrontation is avoided, however, in various ways, and as in many aspects of the language of the child culture, an element of play, and also of humour, serves to blunt the edge of the control mechanism. An obvious example of such humorous control is the use of the put-off. This traditional device, used mainly when speaking to young children, provides an effective means of control while avoiding the tensions and difficulties of direct confrontation. Put-offs are used especially to discourage children from pestering adults with questions thought to be unnecessary, or embarrassing. They use word-play, metaphor and nonsense expressions to deter the child, usually by puzzling him so that he is diverted from his original intention. A few examples will best illustrate this device. When children in the Sheffield family ask their father to play football with them at a time when he is busy or does not want to play, he replies, 'I can't, I've got a bone in my leg.' When the children keep asking, 'Where are you going?', the mother replies, 'To see a man about a dog,' or 'There and back to see how far it is', 'To see my Aunt Fanny,' or 'Off to Timbuctoo.' When a child asks, 'How old are you, Mummy?' the stock response is, 'As old as my tongue and a bit older than my teeth.' 'Where are you, Mummy?' is responded to with, 'I'm in my skin.' When children fail to check facts and say they *thought* something was the case when it was not so, the usual retort is, 'You know what Thought did? He only thought he did.' A more elaborate and picturesque form of this,

52

not used in the Sheffield family, but well known in the city and the surrounding area is, 'You know what Thought did? He followed a muck cart and thought it was a wedding.' The amusing and incongruous comparison emphasizes the need for the child to check his facts and use his powers of observation.

Many put-offs are used to deflect children's questions about food. If a child asks what is for dinner, the reply may be, 'Steam pasty'; 'Few broth'; 'Bread and pullet (pull it)'; 'Toughened dumplings out o' t' pan'; 'Fresh air and snowballs'; or 'A run round t' table and a kick at t' cellar door'. A much more direct reply is, 'What you get, and like it too,' which is an overt control device similar to a threat. The effect of such put-offs is to puzzle the child sufficiently to divert him from his questioning. Some of the most linguistically complex examples, typified by nonsense words and phrases which often give the illusion of sense, are found in answer to such general questions as, 'What is that?' Answers include: 'Layoes for meddlers'; 'A whimwham from mustard town'; 'A wingwam for a goose's bridle'; 'A whimwham to wind mustard mills up with.' If the child asks what these phrases mean they are simply repeated with no further explanation.

The most overt and direct forms of traditional verbal social control are to be found in threats, commands and appeals. Of these, the commands and appeals have already received considerable attention.[16] Commands, or imperative modes of control, as Bernstein refers to them, are typical of the positional type of control.[17] In positional families,

'social control is affected [sic. effected?] either through power or through referring behaviour to universal or particular norms which regulate status. In person-oriented families social control is likely to be realized through verbally elaborated means oriented to the person, while in positional families social control is likely to be realized through less elaborated verbal means, less oriented to the person but more oriented toward the formal status of the regulated (i.e. the child).'[18]

From the first few months of a child's life he may be prepared, and indeed to some extent conditioned, to respond to commands aimed at controlling his behaviour. In the Sheffield family, for example, and in lower- and lower-middle-class families in the area, the very young child's behaviour in certain contexts is effectively controlled by a very limited number of specific linguistic forms, pronounced in an unusual way and often accompanied by specific gestures and other paralinguistic features. When adults in the Sheffield family scold a very young child, they may use the alveolar/dental clicking sounds already referred to above. Alternatively they pronounce the diphthong [o : u], the first element having a time span of some two or three seconds, and the whole diphthong accompanied by voiced pharyngeal and velar friction expressing strong disapproval. This same pharyngeo-velar friction[19] is also used when adults speak to each other in contexts of disapproval, but its function in the verbal social control of children is much more radical. In the child culture it serves as a distinguishing feature of the pronunciation of what Raum, in describing child-rearing in East Africa, designates 'conditioning terms'. Among the Chaga of Tanzania these are words 'uttered in a stentorian voice in certain situations'.[20] In the context of English child-rearing such terms, usually characterized by pharyngeo-velar friction, are used in similar control situations with the same aims and effects. To some degree, these conditioning terms or terms of constraint are used in a similar way in some working-class and lower-middle-class English families 'to create in the child automatically working checks activated in certain situations.'[21] If in the Sheffield family, for example, a preverbal child tries to touch or play with something dirty, his action evokes a loud 'Agh!' [aʕ] (often lengthened to [aːʕ]) from the mother. The sudden loud pronunciation of this sound, with its strong pharyngeo-velar friction, has the effect of startling the child so that he pauses, and this alone gives the mother the opportunity to take some action to prevent him touching the offending substance (excrement, mud, etc.). At a later stage the child himself learns the term and repeats it in appropriate contexts, indicating its speedy impact on both his receptive and expressive skills. Often the term is accompanied by the word dirty, also pronounced by the adult with strong pharyngeo-velar friction. The unusual quality of this sound, which is not part of the phonemic system of English, gives it a distinctiveness which is fully exploited in such contexts of social control. If a very young child crawls towards a fire or a radiator, for example, the mother in the Sheffield family says, 'Burn! Burn him!' using the same fricative sound simultaneously with all the vowel sounds pronounced. The preverbal child is too young and too inexperienced for person-oriented appeals or explanations about the dangers of the fire to have any effect. The use of such terms of constraint is also particularly efficacious if the mother is some distance away from the child, or is engaged in some activity such

54

as baking, which hinders or prevents her from intercepting him before he reaches the danger. The same fricative sound may be added to the pronunciation of many other words in the context of direct control. Typical of such usages is the word n̲o̲, pronounced with an exaggeratedly long diphthong accompanied by the fricative quality. A somewhat different use of the distinctive pharyngeo-velar sound is found in the context of toilet training. To encourage the very young child to 'use the potty' mothers sometimes mime the overt physical efforts required, and at the same time emphasize these efforts by pronouncing sounds such as [ɑʕ], thus offering the preverbal child an imitative model on which to pattern his behaviour.

An interesting group of conditioning terms is characterized not only by pharyngeo-velar friction but also by initial labial sounds. As mentioned earlier, labial sounds, and bilabials in particular, are not only more 'visible' but are frequently used or mimed by adults in communicative interaction with very young children. The possibility that labio-velarity in English words may carry derogatory connotations has recently been the subject of investigation.[22] One might take this notion a step further by considering the origin and development of certain clusters of words across the Indo-European languages which share a remarkably close-knit set of semantic relationships. The etymological interrelationship of these words has been discussed elsewhere,[23] but it is useful to note here that a number of words beginning with /bu/, /pu/, /bo/, /po/, /bɔ/, /pɔ/, among many others with initial labials, frequently denote unpleasant or frightening concepts, or figures of fear. In English, for example, slang and/or baby talk forms such as p̲o̲o̲p̲ (faeces); b̲o̲o̲, b̲o̲o̲b̲o̲, etc., have unpleasant connotations, and b̲u̲g̲a̲b̲o̲o̲, b̲o̲g̲e̲y̲(man), b̲o̲g̲g̲a̲r̲d̲, b̲o̲g̲l̲e̲, etc. denote frightening supernatural figures referred to in threats addressed to children.

Young children may become acquainted with this initial sound group at the preverbal stage of their development. An obvious example of this is the widespread use in English of the word b̲o̲h̲ in games of peek-a-boo with very young children. In such games an adult or older sibling peeps from behind some object, or some location where he is unseen by the child, thrusts his head in the child's direction, adopts the exaggerated facial expression already described (eyebrows raised, eyes opened wide, lips protruding) and says [bɑʕ]. When pronounced in this context of play the word usually amuses the child, although the amusement is often mixed with a degree of surprise or apprehension. If the person appears suddenly or says the word very loudly, the very young child is often startled and his reaction is to cry rather than to laugh or smile. This delicate balance between amusement and fear is typical of many language games used by adults to initiate various aspects of the socialization process. The word boh, for example, has some frightening connotations for the child. Although these are presented in play and as pleasurable in the early stages of his life, the phonetic similarity between boh and the initial syllables in the names of such figures as the bogeyman, later perhaps to be used to threaten the child, is not insignificant. Although the word boh is not a direct conditioning term in comparison, for example, with agh, it is uttered in specific memorable contexts of play, and its more frightening connotations may persist in the child's imagination. The memory of this sound and its connotations may well have been linked with the names of such threatening figures as the bogeyman in English, and more obviously, in regional dialects (e.g. boo-man), as well as in other Germanic languages (e.g. German Bumann).

A much rarer term, well attested in Yorkshire and the neighbouring counties in the early years of this century but now rapidly disappearing, is the word bobba [ˈbɔbɑː], which is still used in the Sheffield family. It is used as a conditioning term when speaking to children and also persists at a facetious level among adults. Perhaps because it is used exclusively in such contexts it is not always pronounced with pharyngeo-velar friction, although this characteristic fricative articulation is used when the situation calls for relatively forceful verbal controls. The term has a universal frame of reference in that it expresses a warning to the child to refrain from acting in any way unacceptable to the adult. If a child touches or attempts to touch some dangerous or fragile thing, for example, he is restrained by the sharp articulation of the word bobba, often reinforced by a gentle tap with the finger on the child's wrist. Irrespective of any interrelationship between words beginning with bilabials /u/, /o/, /ɔ/, etc., this term is used explicitly to control the child's behaviour by developing a kind of conditioned response, and the accompanying tap on the wrist, delivered either playfully or with ominous sharpness, prefigures the possibility of physical punishment.

It is against such a background of rudimentary conditioning and control in the early stages of a child's development that the use of threats in social control is best described and evaluated. Whereas commands and appeals normally entail no expressed

56

retributive consequences for disobedience, threats explicitly state that disobedience will incur retribution. The threats addressed to children in the context of social control display a remarkably restricted patterning on both the structural and the semantic levels. Structurally they consist of three principal classes:

(1) AFFIRMATION
(2) CONDITION + CONSEQUENCE
(3) IMPERATIVE.

Each class is characterized by a 'favourite'[24] structure but may include several sub-categories. An AFFIRMATION is a neutral or unmarked category typified by an affirmative statement, e.g.

(The) ——————— will get you!
(I) will (smack) you!
(The) ——————— is coming!

Threats with this structure predominate over the other classes in the pilot studies undertaken through the Survey of Language and Folklore and also in a full-scale research project on such usages in Newfoundland which I carried out between 1966 and 1972. An interesting sub-category in this class is the threat uttered in the form of a question, e.g. 'Do you want me to give you a smack?' which apparently offers the child some slight element of choice which all the other threats deny him.

The CONDITION + CONSEQUENCE structural class is a positive or marked category consisting of two interrelated elements. The first of these is typified by a conditional clause, and the second is an affirmative statement of a consequence which will ensue if the condition remains unfulfilled. Typical threats of this kind are:

CONDITION	CONSEQUENCE
If you { don't be good / are naughty / say that again	{ the policeman will take you away / you'll get a smack / I'll tell your father

The order of the two elements may be reversed as an optional transformation. This structural class has interesting parallels with the INTERDICTION + VIOLATION + CONSEQUENCE motifemes defined by Dundes.[25]

The IMPERATIVE class is of particular interest in the parallels and contrasts which it offers with Bernstein's 'imperative' category. When commands such as, 'Shut up!'; 'Go to your room!'; 'Get out of my sight!' are used in the context of social control, they would be classed as 'imperatives' by Bernstein and also in the tentative classification presented here. When such an imperative, however, is followed by an affirmative statement of an alternative, reason or result, structurally and semantically linked to it, the designation 'imperative' alone is insufficient. In addition the second element in such structures frequently takes the form of a threat. Three sub-categories of the IMPERATIVE are as follows:

1. IMPERATIVE + ALTERNATIVE, e.g. 'Shut up or I'll smack you!'
2. IMPERATIVE + REASON, e.g. 'Don't go out in the dark because Jack the Ripper is out there!'
3. IMPERATIVE + RESULT, e.g. 'Just you dare do that again and you'll be in trouble!'

Threat structures in each of the three major classes are freely combined into composites:

IMP.   COND. + CONS.

'Shut up this minute! If you don't shut up, I'll get the wooden

A   IMP.

spoon! Do you want me to get it? Well, shut up then!.'

The structural patterns of the various classes of threats and their potential composite forms can be expressed as follows:

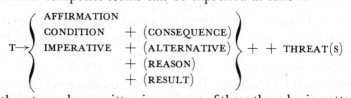

A threat may be rewritten in any one of these three basic patterns. Additional threat structures are allowed for by the incorporation of a cycle rule in the formula. The small number of typical structural patterns indicates the traditional nature of the threats. Like proverbs and other traditional usages within a culture, their characteristic restricted patterning serves not only to identify them and thus help to refine their cultural function, but also to make them memorable so that they persist. Their persistence within a culture, however, also depends upon their relevance, and although the traditional structural patterns have survived, the semantic content of the threats has undergone considerable change in England, especially in the past thirty years. This is particularly obvious in the dramatic decline in the use of supernatural figures in the nominal slots in threats. This decline is due to many different factors,

58

but not least to the influence of popular books for the guidance of mothers in which the use of such figures, and of threats in general, is strongly deprecated. Nevertheless, the threats persist and continue to provide one of the most effective means of verbal social control. Furthermore, they remain linked to the conditioning terms used in the child's earliest months in that the pharyngeovelar friction typical of those spoken terms of constraint is also a common feature of the threats.

The figures used in the threats are typified by certain basic characteristics, either individually or collectively, including, for example, power/authority (actual, imagined or supernatural); abnormality (physical or mental); strangeness; unpredictability; association with unpleasant or dirty things. These threatening figures are of three main types:

1. Supernatural or invented, e.g. God, the Devil, bogeyman, Father Christmas, Jack Frost.
2. Living people, e.g. father, policeman, teacher, murderer, tramp.
3. Animals, e.g. dog, rat.

Preliminary results of the fieldwork indicate very clearly that figures of types 2 and 3 are rapidly superseding those of type 1 in families where threats are in common use at the present time to control children's behaviour. Even so, the threatening figures of type 2 and 3 are often presented as having certain supernatural characteristics typical of the older traditions represented by the type 1 figures.

Both the threats and the figures used in them are part of a complex network of cultural traditions which, among various other functions, continue to play a major role in the social control of children. Many other traditional genres, including folktale, legend, custom and the whole field of children's folklore—especially their sayings, chants, rhymes and games—are a rich source of information on the language of the child culture. As yet these resources have remained largely unexplored. They have much to tell us which is of practical importance not only in the understanding of children's language and traditions but also how this background can be built upon in a more formal educational setting. For the child, the problem of adjusting to such a setting may centre on the change in both the modes and the expression of social control as he moves from the relatively close-knit familial control system into that of the school, and later into that of society as a whole.

In a brief exploratory study such as this it is impossible to do more than hint at the richness and complexity of the language of the child culture as revealed in some of its more obvious forms. Even a cursory study suggests, however, that the patterns and traditions typical of communicative interaction between adults and children in their formative years, make a substantial contribution to the individual child's ability to acquire essential linguistic skills. Equally important is their role in providing guidelines which encourage predictable behaviour and thus play a significant part in his socialization.

Notes

[1] See, for example, Basil Bernstein, *Class, Codes and Control*, 1971 and 1973.
[2] Jenny Cook-Gumperz, *Social Control and Socialization*, 1973.
[3] Bernstein, 'A Sociolinguistic Approach to Socialization,' 1971, 36–41.
[4] Ibid., 46–9.
[5] Ray L. Birdwhistell, *Kinesics and Context*, 1970, p. 6.
[6] Birdwhistell, loc. cit.
[7] Suprasegmental markers are modelled on those of James Sledd, *A Short Introduction to English Grammar*, 1959. Note, however, that sustained terminals are frequently preceded by a slight rise in pitch, irrespective of the immediately following pitch level.
[8] Numerous basic gestures such as nodding, shaking the head, beckoning, etc. are learned by the child in similar imitative contexts.
[9] Fieldwork experience teaches a necessary reluctance to state categorically that such forms are inventions or that they are confined to a specific family. All too often further investigation reveals that they are known and used elsewhere.
[10] Note that postconsonantal [r] is omitted here and in dinky, dinkies, reflecting the difficulty which a young child has in pronouncing such consonant groups, but encouraging him to communicate without the [r] at this early stage before helping him to add it to his expressive inventory later.
[11] This reply is identical with one of the typical verbal social control formulas repeatedly said to children when they behave unacceptably.
[12] The articulation is deliverately exaggerated and is characterized by unusually strong aspiration.
[13] Wayland D. Hand, ed., *Popular Beliefs and Superstitions from North Carolina*, 1961, p. xxxiii.
[14] The potential impact which such folk narratives may have on the child

is considerable. Although too complex a matter to discuss here, cautionary tales, for example, are explicitly intended to encourage the child to behave acceptably.

[15] For a full study of these rain with sunshine dites, see M. Kuusi, *Regen bei Sonnenschein*, 1957.

[16] See, for example, Bernstein, 'A Sociolinguistic Approach,' 41-4.

[17] Ibid., 41.

[18] Loc. cit.

[19] From my own limited kinesthetic observation, this sound is articulated in the section of the vocal tract between the larynx and the velum, the pharynx acting as the principal resonance chamber. The volume and intensity of the sound increase in proportion with the degree of control which the speaker wishes to exercise.

[20] O. F. Raum, *Chaga Childhood*, 1967, p. 237.

[21] Raum, loc. cit.

[22] Roger W. Wescott, 'Labio-Velarity and Derogation in English,' 1971.

[23] J. D. A. Widdowson, 'The Bogeyman: Some Preliminary Observations on Frightening Figures,' 1971.

[24] The term 'favourite' structure is based on C. F. Hockett, *A Course in Modern Linguistics*, 1958, p. 200.

[25] A. Dundes, 'Structural Typology in North American Indian Folktales,' 1965.

Works cited

Bernstein, Basil, *Class, Codes and Control*, 2 vols. London: Routledge and Kegan Paul, 1971 and 1973.

Bernstein, Basil, 'A Sociolinguistic Approach to Socialization: with some Reference to Educability,' Chapter 3 of Frederick Williams, ed., *Language and Poverty: Perspectives on a Theme*. Chicago: Markham Publishing Co., 1971.

Birdwhistell, Ray L., *Kinesics and Context: Essays on Body Motion and Communication*. Philadelphia: University of Pennsylvania Press, 1970.

Cook-Gumperz, Jenny, *Social Control and Socialization: A Study of Class Differences in the Language of Maternal Control*. London: Routledge and Kegan Paul, 1973.

Hand, Wayland D., ed., *Popular Beliefs and Superstitions from North Carolina*, Vol. VI of N. I. White, et. al., eds., *The Frank C. Brown Collection of North Carolina Folklore*. Durham, N.C.: Duke University Press, 1961.

Hockett, C. F., *A Course in Modern Linguistics*. New York: Macmillan, 1958.

Kuusi, Matti, *Regen bei Sonnenschein; zur Weltgeschichte einer Redensart*. Helsinki: Suomalainen Tiedeakatemia, 1957.

Raum, O. F., *Chaga Childhood*, reprint edn. London: Oxford University Press, for the International African Institute, 1967.

Sledd, James, *A Short Introduction to English Grammar*. Chicago: Scott Foresman, 1959.

Wescott, Roger W., 'Labio-Velarity and Derogation in English: A Study in Phonosemic Correlation,' *American Speech*, 46 (1971), 123–37.

Widdowson, J. D. A., 'The Bogeyman: Some Preliminary Observations on Frightening Figures,' *Folklore*, 82 (Summer 1971), 99–115.

3   The language of the mother—child relationship

CATHERINE E. SNOW

By the time children of four or five years go off to school, they know a great deal about the language they speak and about using that language to communicate with others. The process of acquiring this knowledge is, for most children, very fast, relatively painless, and seemingly automatic, so it often goes unnoticed how much time and effort the children themselves and their older caretakers invest in the process. It is the purpose of this paper to look at some of the events and experiences in infancy and early childhood which may contribute to the acquisition of linguistic and communicative skills. These events and experiences include:

1. 'Conversation-like' interactions in early infancy.
2. Having one's first communicative efforts responded to.
3. Receiving linguistic input of a simplified and repetitive nature.
4. Having adults respond to one's signals that their communicative efforts are ineffective.

Whether any or all of these experiences is crucial to normal language development must be further studied.

One of the principles which underlies the view of language acquisition presented here is that language acquisition is the result of an interaction between caretaker (usually, in societies with which we are familiar, the mother) and child in which both play an active role. The role of the child in initiating and in terminating the interaction, in pacing and directing it, and in determining its nature and content is as great as or greater than that of the mother. The mother's contribution to the interaction is that she is uniquely aware of and sensitive to her child's needs, interests, and abilities, and to his special communicative devices. She is

63

therefore in the best position to engage in appropriately paced and mutually interesting interactions with her child.

Reference is continually made in the following discussion to the mother–child relationship, because the mother is the primary caretaker and most constant companion of the young child in the societies where most of the research referred to here has been performed. There is no intention to imply that only the biological mother can perform the caretaker function, nor that she is the best person to perform this function, nor even that one single person can perform it better than two or several.

How mothers and infants communicate

One of the first steps in the child's acquisition of the ability to communicate is learning to signal. Children learn very early that cries of pain, of hunger, and of discomfort are effective in summoning an adult and in changing the situation. Babies in the first three months of life cry more when the mother is far away; by one year they cry more when she is nearby. They have learned that crying communicates and that the addressee must be present for the communication to be effective (Bell & Ainsworth, 1972). Mothers report that they can distinguish different types of cries from one another as early as one month after the baby is born. This assertion is, in fact, probably not true. But it is nonetheless revealing that mothers think it is true, precisely because this means that they are treating their babies, even at this early age, as communicating beings (Eveloff, 1971). As such, mothers set the stage for real communication, creating a situation in which the babies are encouraged to participate actively as soon as they are able to. Similarly, the first time the baby smiles at his mother she can interpret this as communicating that she is recognized as someone special—an attitude which will greatly support later communicative interactions.

But there is a second aspect of the infant's communication system. Infants learn at a very early age that there are rules governing communicative interactions, e.g. that communication involves give and take and that the participants must take turns. Infants seem to have mastered the *form* of communicative interactions long before they can do anything about introducing content to those interactions.

Infants' first experience of communicative interactions comes in the form of 'conversation-like interactions'. What are conversation-like interactions exactly? One example is the 'protoconversation' (Bateson, 1971), an interaction sequence which looks very much like conversation between two adults, in that (a) the two participants look at each other, (b) only one of them talks at a time, (c) when one stops talking, the other begins almost immediately, and (d) each listens to the other. But a typical adult conversation follows lines like the following:

A: Hi, how are things?
B: Well, I got fired last week.
A: Oh dear.
B: But I got a new job.
A: Oh yeah? Is it working out?
B: Pretty well. It's hard work, but twice the salary of the other place.
A: Hey, have they got an opening for me?

whereas a typical protoconversation consists of:

M: What you gonna say?
B: (babbles)
M: Huh?
B: (babbles)
M: Oh dear.
B: (babbles)
M: You gonna be a good boy today?
B: (babbles)
M: (laughs) You're not?

The baby could not contribute much in the way of content to this interaction (quoted from Bateson, 1971); he was only three months old and did not have much to say yet. But he *was able* to sustain an interaction that had many of the characteristics of adult conversations.

Similarly, sequences of gazing at each other by mothers and babies can be described by the same mathematical model used to describe adults talking to each other (Jaffe, Stern, & Perry, 1973).

It would seem that babies, long before the onset of speech, have general rules for communicative interactions. These rules have the chance to develop or be learned because babies are born with a strong tendency to be interested in 'talking, moving faces'. When awake, babies tend to quieten down and pay attention when their mothers come within sight and/or start to talk (Jones & Moss, 1971). This quiet, attentive baby is then ripe to engage in a conversation-like interaction with his mother. If he happens to vocalize while his mother is looking at him or talking to him, she is quite likely to respond with more talking or with attention of some other kind. By the age of three months, babies' productions of vocalizations can be increased if their vocalizations are rewarded by social responses (being touched, spoken to, or looked at) (Jones & Moss, 1971). So all that is needed to create a protoconversation is a baby that is interested in talking adults and an adult who is interested in vocalizing babies. The product of these complementary interests is a child who approaches the language-learning situation with a great deal of knowledge about how to use the language he has not yet learned.

It is of course the case that some adults are less interested in vocalizing babies than others. Fathers, for instance, tend to interact with their infants, and to talk to them, much less than mothers do, an average of 38 seconds per day according to one American study (Rebelsky & Hanks, 1971). This is of course partly a question of opportunity in societies where fathers go to work and mothers stay home. But it is also no doubt a question of cultural norms; women are supposed to be more interested in babies, and are supposed to show their interest and affection more openly, than men. It is acceptable for women to do 'silly' things like talking to infants who are clearly too young to understand. This is somewhat less acceptable for men, and not at all to be expected of them. Therefore infants are mostly dependent on their mothers to teach them about interacting.

But there also exist cultures and subcultures which put little value on interacting with infants. Even two cultures as similar as middle-class America and middle-class Holland differ considerably in their norms for interacting with infants. Dutch mothers tend to believe that young babies should be fed on schedule, should sleep a great deal, should not be overstimulated with crib toys or play sessions, and should not be spoiled (Rebelsky, 1967).

As a consequence of these culturally determined child-rearing norms, Dutch babies (at least up to an age of three months) have considerably less interaction with their mothers than American babies, and the interactions that do occur tend to be initiated and scheduled by the mother rather than by the baby. Dutch mothers show much less tendency to respond to fussing or crying babies than do American mothers, nor do they exploit openings for conversation-like interactions as often. Nonetheless, Dutch babies do grow up normally and do learn to talk. Does this mean that

66

mother–infant interaction at a few months of age has no effect on later language acquisition? Nobody knows, because no one has directly related the speed or ease of language learning in children from different child-rearing cultures to the opportunities for pre-linguistic conversation-like interactions within the cultures. How-ever, it has been shown that the IQ scores of 8–10 month old in-fants whose mothers were restrictive and engaged in little physical or verbal contact were lower than those of infants whose mothers were permissive and engaged in much verbal and physical con-tact. This difference was found even within a group of middle-class mothers, all of whom provided fully adequate and loving maternal care (Beckwith, 1971). This effect of maternal style on IQ strongly suggests that maternal style in first several months of life could also affect the course of language acquisition which occurs a year and a half later.

Just as Dutch mothers think it is overstimulating to play too much with their young infants, lower-class American mothers think it is ludicrous to talk to somewhat older children (Tulkin & Kagan, 1972). Middle-class mothers tend to report of their pre-linguistic children that they 'can't talk very well yet, but she under-stands everything I say to her'. This belief is probably as incorrect as the belief that one-month-old babies produce distinguishable cries, and it may well support the child's learning to communicate in a similar way. Because mothers believe their children can understand them, they talk to them. Because they believe their children are already learning to talk, they teach them words and play verbal games with them. Thus the child can start learning language as soon as his cognitive capacities allow him to, and even before that time he has had much practice in listening to language and in learning that spoken words carry messages. He is thus acquiring the communicative skills which make the job of acquir-ing linguistic skills much easier. The lower-class child whose mother thinks him (probably correctly) too young to talk or to understand misses a huge chunk of experience which may well speed up the language acquisition process.

How mothers talk to children

We have in the first section discussed generally how mothers inter-act with their infants. We have seen that such factors as responding to an infant's crying, providing him with toys, playing with him, looking at him, talking to him, and responding when he smiles or vocalizes, all play a role in early mother–infant interactions, and may have an effect on the later development of language. We will now look more specifically at one aspect of mother–child interaction that intuitively would seem to be the most important for language development—how mothers talk to their children.

The issue of how mothers talk to their children has become very important to the study of developmental psycholinguistics because of its relevance to the nativism–empiricism controversy. Nativists such as Chomsky and others see language as a process of unfolding or discovery; they stress how complicated a system language is, that attempts to teach non-humans to talk have failed, that the process of language development is very similar for all children no matter what language they are learning, that language development is closely related to maturational milestones for innate motoric development, and that the structure of the linguistic system is not directly derivable from a list of utterances. The first and last points are really central to the argument; not only is language a very complex system, but it is a system whose structure is obscured in the spoken language we hear, which is often confused, garbled, poorly constructed, and inadequately organized. Because the language they hear gives them so little real information about the structure of the language which they will have to learn, children must have innate linguistic abilities which enable them to recognize the underlying structure despite the confusing input. That is, according to the nativists.

The empiricists or behaviourists point out that although adult language is a complex system, the language children learn to speak is considerably simpler. Furthermore, they say, the language children hear is not garbled, confused or misleading—it is very well organized to be quite transparent in structure even to a young child. Empiricists emphasize that environmental factors play an important role in how quickly and how well children learn to talk, and that language acquisition takes a long time and is characterized by much explicit teaching on the part of the mother and implicit practice on the part of the child. According to the empiricists all this means that language is learned just as other skills are learned. Innate characteristics which are prerequisite to that learning may exist, but then they are general characteristics like being social, finding human beings interesting, wishing to be able to communicate, recognizing that objects can be categorized, etc., not specific linguistic universals like knowing that sentences have subjects and predicates, or knowing that there are different gram-

68

matical classes of words. It is not our purpose here to discuss the nativist–empiricist controversy at length—nor would that be very fruitful, since both positions are more 'ways of looking at things' than they are statements of truth. The controversy is important in the present context primarily because it has been the motivation for detailed description of the speech of mothers to their babies and young children by experimenters seeking to support the empiricist claims. These data will provide the basis for the discussion to follow.

Baby-Talk

The phenomenon of baby-talk—'It's an itsy-bitsy cutie-pie, isn't it?'—is one which we all recognize and occasionally shudder at. Baby-talk is a phenomenon which belongs to the culture of child-raising; in some cultures it is considered the appropriate way to address small children. In other cultures it is seen as demeaning and potentially harmful to the child. Nonetheless, despite cultural norms, it is probably safe to say that all cultures have some baby-talk forms. Baby-talk has, furthermore, some characteristics which are very similar no matter what the adult language is. Consonant cluster simplification or substitution, for example, is typical of baby-talk in English (tummy for stomach) as well as in Dutch (noepie for snoepje, sweetie), Comanche American Indian (píhI for kwíhI, wife, and pánA for kwánA, smell) and Papiamentu Spanish (panu for aeroplanu, airplane).

Syllable reduplication and onomatopoetic or rhyming words are also common (English: yum-yum for delicious, itsy-bitsy for little; Dutch: woef-woef for dog; French: do-do for dormir; Comanche: tutú for train; Berber: duddu for udi, butter; and the ubiquitous pipi for urinate). There is a tendency to use diminutive endings widely (English: -ie or -y, as in doggie and nappy; Dutch: -ie or -je; Comanche: -cí as in haicí, friend) (Bynon, 1968; Casagrande, 1968; Ferguson, 1964). Pronouns show certain deviations from normal usage, e.g., 'Are we hungry?' for 'Are you hungry?', 'Isn't it a cute baby?' for 'Aren't you a cute baby?', and 'Mama's going now' for 'I'm going now' (Wills, 1974). The voice is pitched higher than normal in baby-talk, and the normal intonation patterns are greatly exaggerated.

In terms of grammatical structure and content, the speech addressed to babies up to about a year of age is widely variant. Some mothers produce quite complicated monologues, though maintaining baby-talk intonation patterns, probably on the assumption that the baby will not understand anyway. Other mothers adapt the content and the structural characteristics of their speech to the baby's limited abilities very early (Phillips, 1973). Examples of monologues that might be produced by these two kinds of mothers follow:

1. And what are we gonna do when daddy gets home? Maybe we should go buy a big steak at the supermarket and grill it outdoors on the barbecue. Hmm? Would you like that?

2. Pretty baby. It's such a pretty baby. How is pretty baby today? Hungry? Are you hungry? Do you want your bottle? We'll go get you a bottle. Just a minute. Wait just a minute.

In neither of these cases would the mothers really expect the baby to understand, or to respond. The first mother has chosen to think aloud about reasonable adult topics, whereas the second has limited her topics to baby-oriented ones, and has produced grammatically much simpler sentences.

Semantic restrictions

This variation and free choice in the sometimes quite complicated monologues disappears by the time the baby is 18 months old; at that time all mothers—indeed, all adults—address children in a grammatically very simple way about a severely restricted set of topics. These topics can be described as limited to 'everydayness', the 'here-and-now', concrete concepts (Phillips, 1973). Mothers tend to talk to children about what the children themselves are doing, about the objects they are looking at, holding, or playing with, about what is going on around them. Discussions about what happened yesterday or what will happen tomorrow are relatively infrequent, and if they do occur tend to be practised routines of the following sort:

M: Who is coming next week?
C: Santa Claus
M: What will he ride in?
C: Sleigh
M: And what is he bringing?
C: Toys
M: Who are the toys for?
    etc.

The fact that mothers limit the topics of their conversations with

70

children to a fairly small set of shared experiences may be crucial in the development of language. A theory of language acquisition has been presented which is based on precisely this assumption—that children can learn to talk only because the meaning of the vast majority of utterances they hear is obvious. This theory, which has been called the theory of Semantic Primacy, sees the language development process as one led and controlled by the child's cognitive development (see Macnamara, 1972). Children first learn to understand the world, to identify objects, to categorize, to recognize cause and effect; once the children have recognized and understood the important facts about reality, they can begin to correlate certain facts or states or occurrences with certain maternal utterances. Thus, a mother's sentence 'That is a dog' can provide information to a child about (1) the appropriate word for a concept and (2) the syntactic form for sentences with a labelling function. But the child could not use that information, would not be able to understand nor process it, if he did not already have the concept for which he was searching for a name. The majority of mothers' utterances can be seen as having this sort of function, namely describing events which the child has just experienced and thereby giving him names for his concepts, e.g. 'Your milk is all gone' to a child who has just emptied his glass, 'Daddy's coming home' as the car pulls into the driveway, or 'It is time for lunch' as the child is placed in his high chair. Mothers' utterances can be seen as the linguistically simplest description of the most salient aspects of the current situation. Mothers say what their children are most likely to be thinking about any situation. Thus does the meaning of maternal utterances remain transparent, and does the child have a chance to learn how his own thoughts must be expressed in the adult language.

No one has ever directly tested the Semantic Primacy theory of language acquisition, nor would it be morally feasible to test it by, for example, giving a child as his only linguistic input four hours a day of reading from the *Encyclopedia Britannica*. However, there is some evidence that children whose 'ways of organizing the world', as revealed in the first fifty words they choose to learn, do not match their mothers' views of the world, as revealed in the kinds of words they use most often, learn language with greater difficulty than children whose mothers' cognitive organizations do match their own (Nelson, 1973). Thus, it would seem that children start with a set of concepts for which they search for names in the linguistic input. If their mothers think the same kinds of concept important, then they will naturally provide the correct names in the course of their comments on what is happening around the child. But if the mother has different ideas about what is important—if she, for example, persists in commenting 'He says bow-wow' about a picture of a dog, while the child wants to know the name for the class of dogs,—then the child's language acquisition will be slowed down.

Linguistic input to children is, thus, usually characterized by being semantically interpretable: that is, able to be understood by the child at any given level of development; in those cases where it is not entirely interpretable, language acquisition is impeded. But mothers' speech to children has other striking characteristics besides its here-and-nowness. It is also grammatically very simple, is highly redundant with the same thing being said in many different ways, and shows particular intonation patterns. These characteristics will be treated in the following sections.

Grammatical simplicity

There are many different ways of measuring grammatical simplicity in speech—but on all the different measures used in several different studies of mothers' speech to children, mothers speak more simply to children than to adults, and more simply to younger children than to older children (see Broen, 1972; Phillips, 1973; Remick, 1972; Snow, 1972a). Mean or average length of utterance, which is the most generally used and perhaps most useful measure of linguistic complexity in young children, is always in the range three to eight words per utterance in speech addressed to two-year-old children, whereas for older children and adults it ranges from eight to ten. Mean length of utterances in itself says nothing, of course, about precisely what makes sentences long and complex. A more detailed analysis of those structures that make sentences long and complex, such as subordinate clauses and co-ordinations, reveals that they are either very infrequent or entirely absent in the speech of mothers to young children.

Other optional structures in sentences, such as adjectives, adverbs and prepositional phrases of various sorts, are used in mothers' speech, but at a rate of one or at most two per sentence. In general, sentences are pared down to one idea, and that idea is expressed as simply as possible in terms of grammar.

72

A large number of the sentences addressed by mothers to their young children are 'labelling sentences', of the form 'That is a ——————' or 'This is a——————'. These sentences are, of course, of the utmost grammatical simplicity. Mothers also use imperatives a great deal when talking to two-year-olds—and there is some indication that lower-class mothers use them more often than middle-class mothers (Snow et al., 1974). Imperatives can be very simple sentences, e.g. 'Get your gloves', 'Pick up the dollie', and 'Drink your milk'. Questions, which at least in English are quite complex to produce, are used much more often in speech to two-year-olds than with older children or adults (Sachs, Brown & Salerno, 1972; Snow et al., 1974); however, it is to a large extent fairly simple questions which are posed, most often 'What is that?'. These questions, which are quite simple grammatically, are nonetheless sometimes quite complex in that the communicative force is very different from what it would be in adult language. 'What is that?', for example, which would be used to an adult as a request for information, is almost exclusively used to children in situations in which the speaker knows the answer perfectly well, i.e. with a tutorial function. Similarly, 'Are your hands clean?' when addressed to a child means 'Wash your hands' and 'Are you sleepy?' very often means 'You're sleepy!'.

Many aspects of the grammatical simplicity of maternal speech are clearly a result of the semantic limitations discussed above. Discussions of the here-and-now make no reference to the past or future, so the tense system is largely limited to the present, and temporal subordinate clauses such as 'When you have done this, go and do ...' are also unnecessary. Describing what is going on at the moment requires minimal use of subordinate clauses introduced by if, unless, because, although, or as a result of. Grammatical functions are limited to the bare minimum—subject, verb, direct object, place adverbials, and a few more. New ones are added only as the child shows the ability to understand them and the need to use them himself.

Redundancy

Mothers talking to two-year-olds never seem to say anything just once. Words and phrases as well as whole sentences are repeated again and again. The type-token ratio, a measure of the diversity of vocabulary used in a text or conversation, has been found to be in the range .3 to .5 for speech to two-year-olds, as compared

73

to .5 to .7 in speech to adults (Broen, 1972; Phillips, 1973). Children hear a relatively small number of words over and over again—a fact which must help them immensely in the difficult task of segmenting the stream of speech they hear into meaningful units. Furthermore, children hear phrases from sentences repeated out of context and in new contexts, as in the following passage:

Put the red truck in the box. The red truck. That's right, in the box. Put it in the box. Come on, the red one. The red one. In the box. Put it in there.

Nativists in the language acquisition controversy have long contended that children must have built-in information about language, because they would otherwise never analyse for themselves the complex hierarchical organization of sentences, represented by some linguists in tree diagrams like the following:

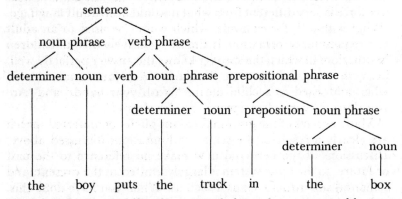

Repetition sequences like that quoted above, however, could serve to isolate constituents of the sentence, and then to show how smaller constituents added together make up larger constituents, e.g.,

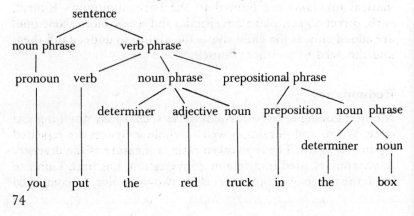

Repetition is not all of this constituent-juggling type, of course. Sometimes it consists of a mother saying one thing in several ways, presumably because the child shows insufficient responsiveness to or comprehension of the original version. This production of paraphrases is clearly controlled by one of the major principles of mother–child interaction: the child must understand what is said to him. Children are not allowed not to understand; and their comprehension is ensured (a) by trying to express only simple ideas, (b) by phrasing the simple ideas in simple ways, and (c) by carefully monitoring the child's response so that they can be said a different way if the first seems ineffective.

Intonation Patterns or Prosody

As in baby-talk, mothers' speech to children is higher pitched than normal speech, and shows an exaggerated intonation pattern (Garnica, 1974; Remick, 1972). The higher pitch is probably used because it attracts children's attention. In fact, even very young babies are more attentive to a female than to a male voice (Brazelton, quoted in Korner, 1973). It may be that the attraction of a high-pitched voice for children is built-in, or it may be that they learn that high-pitched speech is addressed to them and that they should listen. It is in either case a very handy mechanism; it means that children know what is for them, and that they do not even have to try to figure out what adults are saying to each other in the early stages of language acquisition. If no such mechanism existed for making 'child-speech' clearly distinguishable from 'adult-speech', children might try to learn to talk on the basis of highly inappropriate linguistic data, the relatively complex speech of adults to adults, and might become quite confused in the process.

The exaggerated intonation contour typical of adult-child speech has two potential functions:

1. It causes the content words in the sentence to be even more heavily stressed than normal. It is, of course, the content words, not the unstressed grammatical function words, which are crucial to the child in deciphering the message. Thus, the exaggerated intonation is a way of making the semantic content of the speech clearer.

2. The exaggerated contour makes it easier for the child to correlate syntactic form with meaning. Questions, imperatives, and statements are made very highly recognizable sentence types,

75

since the intonation pattern associated with each is even more distinctive than in normal speech. Thus, the child can recognize on prosodic grounds what kind of sentence is being offered, and can then search for the syntactic markers (word order, wh-words, or whatever) which occur in conjunction with each intonation pattern.

How children influence their mothers

All of these modifications in mothers' speech for young children—the restriction of semantic content, the redundancy, the intonation, the grammatical simplification—are adjusted to the level of the child. Though a child of two and a child of three will both be addressed with modified speech styles, the speech addressed to the two-year-old will be even simpler and more redundant so that the same thing is said in more than one way, than the speech addressed to the three-year-old. How do mothers know exactly what level speech to produce for their children at every age and at every stage of development? They know because the children tell them, using various cues of less or greater subtlety.

Children become less attentive when the speech addressed to them does not show the normal characteristics of maternal speech (Snow, 1972b; Dale, 'Personal Communication').

They become less likely to respond when the sentences addressed to them begin with words they do not know (Shipley, Gleitman & Smith, 1969). Furthermore, children of course share with adults certain techniques for modifying the speaker's style,—such as saying 'What?' or 'Huh?' or 'This one?' or other such explicit expressions of noncomprehension. Adults seem to be very sensitive to all these various cues from children, and to keep modifying their speech styles until the inattention, the lack of comprehension, and the questioning disappear. Thus, the production of appropriately modified speech styles for young children is the result of a process of interaction based on mutual expectations to communicate on the part of both mother and child.

The child's tendency to stop listening when speech becomes too complex has a second effect, besides that of causing the adult to change his speech style. The child's attentional system functions as a filter which passes only appropriate linguistic data. Sentences which begin with unfamiliar words, sentences whose syntactic form is indecipherable and whose semantic content is unclear, never get through the filter. Thus, an adult who is exceptionally

76

unskilled in adjusting his speech to the abilities of the child, or who is unusually obtuse in picking up the child's signals of inattention and noncomprehension, will not be able to retard the child's language acquisition process. The inappropriate sentence, which might have confused the child and complicated his language-learning task, simply does not get through.

Learning to talk

By the time children are four to five years old, they have learned to talk well enough to use language in much the same way adults do—for transferring information and ideas, for making contact with other people, and for inducing others to do what you want them to do. This achievement is possible because the child has learned a great deal about language as a means of communication, and about language as an abstract system characterized by complicated and sometimes arbitrary rules of syntax and morphology. This second kind of learning—learning the rules of syntax—is dependent on the first kind, and gives relatively little trouble precisely because the first kind has already taken place, at least partially.

Children come to the language-learning situation with the expectation that meaningful things will be said to them, and mothers fulfil that expectation beautifully. Similarly, mothers expect their children to try to communicate, and respond immediately to any behaviour that can be interpreted as communicative. Thus arises an interaction which leads to true communication, and which along the way provides the model opportunity for learning the rules of grammar.

References

Bateson, M. C. 'Epigenesis of conversational interaction', paper presented to the Society for Research in Child Development, Minneapolis, 1971.

Beckwith, L. 'Relationships between attributes of mothers and their infants' IQ scores', *Child Development*, *42*, 1971, 1083–98.

Bell, S. & Ainsworth, M. 'Infant crying and maternal responsiveness', *Child Development*, *43*, 1972, 1171–90.

Broen, P. A. 'The verbal environment of the language-learning child', American Speech and Hearing Association Monograph no. 17, December 1972.

Bynon, J. 'Berber nursery language', Transactions of the Philological Society, 1968, 107–61.

Casagrande, J. B. 'Comanche Baby Talk', International Journal of American Linguistics, 14, 1968, 11–14.

Eveloff, H. 'Some cognitive and affective aspects of early language development', Child Development, 42, 1971, 1895–1907.

Ferguson, C. A. 'Baby talk in six languages', in J. J. Gumperz and D. Hymes (eds.), 'The ethnography of communication', American Anthropologist, 66, 1964, No. 6, part 2, 103–14.

Garnica, O. 'Some prosodic characteristics of speech to young children', paper presented at Conference on Language Input and Acquisition, Boston, September, 1971.

Jaffe, J., Stern, D., & Perry, J. ' "Conversational" coupling of gaze behavior in prelinguistic human development', Journal of Psycholinguistic Research, 2, 1973, 321–30.

Jones, S. & Moss, H. 'Age, state, and maternal behavior associated with infant vocalisations', Child Development, 42, 1971, 1039–52.

Korner, A. F. 'Early stimulation and maternal care as related to infant capabilities and individual differences', Early Child Development and Care, 2, 1973, 307–27.

Macnamara, J. 'Cognitive basis of language learning in infants'. Psychological Review, 79, 1972, 1–13.

Nelson, K. 'Structure and strategy in learning to talk', Society for Research in Child Development Monograph no. 141, 38, 1973, nos. 1 & 2.

Phillips, J. 'Formal characteristics of speech which mothers address to their young children', doctoral dissertation, Johns Hopkins University, 1973.

Rebelsky, F. 'Infancy in two cultures', Nederlands Tijdschrift voor Psychologie, 22, 1967, 27–36.

Rebelsky, F. & Hanks, C. 'Fathers' verbal interactions with infants in the first three months of life', Child Development, 42, 1971, 63–8.

Remick, H. 'Maternal speech to children during language acquisition', paper presented at International Symposium of First Language Acquisition, Florence, Italy, 1972.

Sachs, J., Brown, R. & Salerno, R. 'Adults' speech to children', paper presented at International Symposium on First Language Acquisition, Florence, Italy, 1972.

Shipley, E., Gleitman, L. & Smith, C. 'A study in the acquisition of language: Free responses to commands', Language, 45, 1969, 322–42.

Snow, C. E. 'Mothers' speech to children learning language', Child Development, 43, 1972, 549–65 (a).

Snow, C. E. 'Young children's responses to adult sentences of varying complexity', paper presented at International Conference of Applied Linguistics, Copenhagen, 1972 (b).

Snow, C. E., Arlman-Rupp, A., Hassing, Y., Jobse, J., Joosten, J. & Vorster, J. 'Mothers' speech in three social classes', unpublished paper, Institute for General Linguistics, University of Amsterdam, 1974.

Tulkin, S. & Kagan, J. 'Mother–child interaction in the first year of life', *Child Development*, *43*, 1972, 31–42.

Wills, D. D. 'Participant deixis in English and Childish', paper presented at Conference on Language Input and Acquisition, Boston, September, 1974.

4 The language of teenage groups

CLEM ADELMAN

'They don't speak our language' ... Nowhere has the title of this book been used more frequently than in the context of adults referring to the language of teenage groups. How meaningful is the insight of this 'common-sense' language phrase the reader may assess for himself in the course of this essay.

As the title suggests, I shall consider the notion of the teenage 'group' and the 'language' of the group, but the reader must not expect this to be a simple business. The straightforward title camouflages a multitude of moving targets—targets which themselves are interrelated and which also move historically. I hope to locate some of these moving targets.[1]

Let us begin by looking at four extracts which start the process of examining the series of relationships between values, experience, language usage and group identity which are the subject of this essay:

> MY GENERATION
> People try to put us down
> Just because we get around.
> Things they do look awful cold
> Hope I die before I get old.
> This is my generation, baby.
> Why don't you all f-f-f-fade away
> Don't try and dig what we all say
> I'm not trying to cause a big sensation
> I'm just talking 'bout my generation.
> This is my generation, baby,
> My generation.
>
> Peter Townshend
> (of 'The Who')[2]

'There are many similarities between the Skinheads of the 70s and the Mods of the 60s—they tend to come from the same sort of council-house background; they veer towards the same uniformity of dress (the girls' drab two-tone suits of last winter echoing the Mod girls below-the-knee skirts of the winter 1963/1964), and even, in the Spring of 1972, the scooter is making something of a comeback.

But there are differences: the Skinheads were, originally, a reaction against what many of the Mods had become.

'The Mods were dominated by Pop Music and their lifestyle was dictated by it. They had their own groups: the Yardbirds, The Who, The Stones and the Small Faces. They had their own TV show in "Ready Steady Go", compered by their own representative in high places, Cathy MacGowan. They even had their own drugs, in Purple Hearts and other amphetamines. But, all of it sprang from Rock.'[3]

'"So," Mr Leary began, looking once more at Dr Schofield, "do I understand your evidence generally to come to this: that the contents of OZ 28 dealing with drugs and devious sexuality would have an effect upon the minds of young children, but it would not be a harmful one? Does that fairly summarise what you have told us?" he asked Schofield. "Yes," said Schofield. "Do you agree that the School Kids issue relentlessly promotes some elements of the new culture; that is a phrase which is, perhaps, known to you?" Schofield replied: "As I understand it, it was written by schoolchildren; so, to that extent, it reflects the ideas of people of that age."

'"I am suggesting that one of the elements which the magazine promotes is dope?" said Leary smiling. "I'm afraid I don't understand the word 'dope'," replied Schofield, totally incredulously. "Mr Schofield, let me make it abundantly plain. I'm suggesting to you that this magazine relentlessly promotes DOPE. Agree or disagree?"

'"I have to disagree," said Schofield. It was the Leary technique all over again. "Rock 'n' Roll. Agree or disagree?" he asked. "I speak subject to correction," began Schofield, "but I doubt if you'll find the words Rock 'n' Roll in the ..."

'"May I have an answer?" interrupted Leary. "Do you agree or disagree?"

'"I'll have to disagree," said Schofield. "And the final element in the so-called new culture, which has been relentlessly promoted is an element described as 'fucking in the streets'. Agree or disagree?" Leary paused.

81

'Schofield, a former RAF fighter pilot, now employed by the Health Education Council, looked bewildered.'[4]

'Paul Goodman writes:

He (Otto Jespersen) shows that, contrary to expectation, a child does not learn his mother tongue at home from his mother and immediate family, he does not pick up their accent. The accent, vocabulary, syntax, and style that form his speech are learned from his first peer groups, outside the home. Jespersen does not explain it, but the psychology seems evident. Speech occurs at the stage of the developing of the "I", it is a forming of the image of the self, it is a self-appointment to one's ideal and putting on its uniform. Changes occur as we appoint ourselves to one peer group after another. At a certain stage a lad appoints himself or commits himself to a band of friends and puts on its jargon, tattoo, and masculine ring on the fourth finger of the left hand.'[5]

How do we come to recognize what we call a 'group' of people? Is the recognition done for us pointedly, say, by the mass media, or do we have some commonsense ways of differentiating between collections of individuals? Are the occupants of a waiting room to be called a group? What groups have in common is that individuals have certain affiliations to each other. They share certain values and express their particular experiences and interpretations of the world in characteristic talk, of which some very good examples about the topic 'pop' are given in the Rutherford essay in this collection. The Rutherford essay tends to assume that the sharing of certain values which are often hidden from adults by a special kind of referencing device used in speech (Rutherford's notion of unanalysability) is dependent to a large extent upon age grouping. While this is true to a certain degree, other factors, other affiliations, have sometimes prior and more significant claims on the system of teenage values. For example, in some cases, the social class, the religion, the teenage group and so on can be seen to have much more influence on the values of any one teenager. If it is possible to talk in any meaningful way about the language of teenage groups, one aspect which occurs in large measure is that the language of such a group is used by the members of the group deliberately to 'mark themselves off' from *all* adults and other teenagers who are not members of that particular group. That is that the teenagers deliberately develop as a set of individuals in a group a particular way of talking and referencing so that members and non-members can be instantly recognizable. There is the further advantage of making it difficult for an outsider

82

(especially an adult) to catch at the value system embodied in the special language.

Only in the limited sense of being distinguishable in age (approximately 10–20) are 'teenagers' a group. To assert that all teenagers share similar values is not supported by any evidence. The non-teenager's social perceptions, like those which assign affiliations to individuals because of a particular hair-style or adulation of a pop star or footballer, seem to derive more from ignorance and suspicion than from interest and concern. 'Teenagers' are recognizable worldwide:

'Young urbanites in Kinshasa participate in a teenage pop culture which distinguishes them from their seniors in a manner familiar to us from our own society. This culture is permeated by the symbols and mythical figures of the cinema and advertising. A striking feature of it in Kinshasa is the "Cowboys and Indians" motif, of which perhaps the dominant figure is "Buffalo Bill". He and his Indian opponents, who are also taken as symbolic for teenagers, represent the use of force in pursuing individual ambitions. Both cowboys (Buffalo Bill) and Indians fight openly for their aims; for this reason they are also, to a certain extent, asocial beings, representing competitiveness unrestrained by social mores. The names of gangs show a recurrent theme—the collectivity of powerful persons known from mass communications. Some names I collected were: Russians, Cowboys, Indians, Americans, and "Onusiens" (ONU being the French version of UNO). The titles of gang leaders and other officers reflect the theme chosen, although lack of information results in some odd associations: the Onusiens were led by Khrushchev with Kennedy as second-in-command! The name Bill with various additions is a common sobriquet. Teenagers may also refer to themselves as "Indians".' [6]

If they have distinctive experiences and associated descriptive content vocabulary, then it seems possible that the affiliations will be based on geographical proximity, recreational pursuits, social class, religious loyalties, sex, age, and admiration of a common hero or heroine and/or ideology.

In any discussion about a language and the society in which it occurs, or to put it the other way around, in any discussion about a society and its language, there is a large element of the chicken and egg argument. In broad terms first, does the acquisition of a particular maternal language influence the sort of society, the system of values, the ways of thinking and so on that an individual may come to adopt? Or is it the other way around? Does the sort of society have a prior influence on the kind of language and the

83

things that can be coded in language which *then* affect how an individual thinks and what his system of values is? Such a discussion about language and society is generally examined in terms of national languages and national characteristics, but it is also possible to examine it from the point of view of sub-cultures in a larger society.

In looking at the phenomenon of teenage groups, a thorny problem has to be grasped: whether it is the acquisition of the group's language *or* the way of experiencing the world that initiates or allows access to the group, is fundamental to a consideration of the significance of language as a means of bringing about group identity. This problem suffuses the essay; it crosses the bases for affiliation as purveyed above.

Howard Becker's study of initiation into marijuana use makes the point.

'Many new users are ashamed to admit ignorance and, pretending to know already, must learn through the more indirect means of observation and imitation:

"I came on like I had turned on (smoked marijuana) many times before, you know. I didn't want to seem like a punk to this cat. See, like I didn't know the first thing about it—how to smoke it, or what was going to happen, or what. I just watched him like a hawk—I didn't take my eyes off him for a second, because I wanted to do everything just as he did it. I watched how he held it, how he smoked it, and everything. Then when he gave it to me I just came on cool, as though I knew exactly what the score was. I held it like he did and took a poke just the way he did."' [7]

Although the novice knew and used the word 'high' ('to get high'—to experience distinct effects from taking a drug), he did not comprehend the full meaning until he had learnt how to achieve the full experience.

To reiterate a point made above about the complex of relations between language and society and society and language, to be a full member of a particular group means that an individual has to have *both* the necessary special language *and* the underlying system of values. It is not sufficient to have an active use of the special language—with its special vocabulary and set of meanings implying a different set of values, and perhaps distinctive syntax and pronunciation—but an active understanding and acceptance of the group's aims and 'life style' is also needed. This latter is much more difficult for the outsider to come by, for involved in

84

it is active participation in the group's activities which can only happen after an individual teenager is part of the group. It could be that we are back to the chicken and egg dilemma, but in fact this is not the case. There is a way out of the dilemma which is often used, namely some sort of initiation into a group's *mores* and language.

But before we go any further it is worthwhile to explain here three terms which dissect 'language' into more specialized examples:

VERNACULAR: What I refer to as 'the common language'. The parts of the language used by large sections of the *adult* population, as in families.

ARGOT: The language usage of particular, more exclusive groups within the total population. These groups are affiliated through sharing similar values and experiences.

SLANG: A more insular form derived from the vernacular.

JARGON: Technical terms of a work or recreational group which does not necessarily share values.

Although this definition of argot implies an attempt to express the distinctiveness of the group's experiences as perceived and interpreted through values, it is clear that plentiful evidence to support this point of view is difficult to come by. There seems to be only one transcription of talk between group members that is unimpaired by the presence of an interviewer.[8]

Certainly, some mutual trust must have developed between interviewer and group members before 'authentic' talk occurs, that is as if the interviewer were not there. Trust may develop in time after continuous indications by the researcher of interest and non-interference with the group. The participant observer must eventually be able to distinguish 'lame' informants (see p. 87) from 'authentic'. As W. H. Whyte[9] points out, on many days the group doesn't seem to be doing anything specially distinctive and perhaps this is why reporters often have to provide their own 'encouragement' and 'stimulation' to provoke action. Perhaps this is what *Glasgow Gang Observed* lacks.[10] It seems a voyeur's viewpoint in spite of the statements invoking involvement with the group.

It may be difficult for the outsider to grasp the meaning of a single lexical item in its full connotation for the group. Even how the group gets its name is a problem; more than likely it is self-dubbing at the locale of its innovation, but it is quickly spread nationwide by the media, especially newspapers.

85

Argot as a term to describe group talk is more appropriate than language because it suggests a variation of the vernacular characterized by differing lexis and, perhaps, pronunciation. Often, however, the argot has very similar surface features but quite different meaning when used within the group.

I had a little bother (about the difficulty of starting the car in the morning).
I had a little bovver (about being involved in a fight or punch up).

Gone out of this world (in memoriam).
(Real) gone, out of this world (jive talk, about drug effects, argot circa 1940).

I am uptight baby (I feel perfectly in tune with my surroundings and its people—black, inner city, American).
(Am I) uptight baby (I am tense and fraught with anxiety—advertising, mass media, white urban East Coast American).

Let it all hang out (alluding to extent of exposure of penis).
Let it all hang out (hippie or President Nixon—to tell the truth).

Jitterbug (wild dancer to jazz music, especially in the aisles of a theatre during the concert).
Jitterbug (as used by Neville Chamberlain—a frightened or panicky person—the jitters).

Speed kills (road safety poster).
Speed kills (comment on possible effects of an overdose of amphetamines).

There is an impermanence about the lexis of teenage groups which makes it unlike the jargon of the civil service, anglers, the Army, etc. The relative permanence of the jargon of the adult groups mentioned, and many others not mentioned, when compared with the jargon of teenage groups, is a factor of the differing kinds of pressure on the groups. To be a member of an adult group such as anglers or motor racing enthusiasts, one needs to share a common interest or enthusiasm with others quite openly. As the adult groups are relatively open to all those interested enough to want to join, it follows that no one is excluded from membership if he really wants to join. The adult groups which are open share the same system of values as most other groups of adults irrespective of their particular interests. What marks out the separate interest groups is the fact that they have some amount of specialized jargon. But unlike the jargon of teenage groups, the jargon of the adult groups does not embody a different set of values. On
86

the other hand, the impermanence of the jargon of teenage groups is related to the vulnerability of such groups to adult pressures to conformity, both in word and deed—if not thought as well. When the argot becomes publicly known, especially as purveyed by mass media—swinging, hip, rave, cool—the group drops those items of their lexicon and creates others, in order to sustain their distinctiveness from adults and other teenage groups. So what seems to outsiders as fad and fashion and hedonistic seeking after unique experience is a necessity for the sustenance of the group's identity for itself. It must constantly recreate and evolve, yet retain the same basic values. Although costumes and hairstyles change, the underlying modes of affiliation remain stable. Whereas long hair is no longer distinctive of any particular teenage group, the argot that the person with long hair uses is a much more reliable index of affiliation. The crucial issue involved the meaning of words for the group; and their appropriate use in particular social contexts[11] (who, when, where). So 'bovver' has been merely glossed by describing it as a fight or punch up. Here is an extract from a skinhead's account of a spot of 'bovver':

'He must have had some bottle that Max, 'cause all of his mates run away and 'e still came out of the Foresters and started 'itting people. They ripped 'is shirt off and started kicking 'im in the face and you know how when you get kicked in the face you start moaning and ... well, 'e just sort of said nothing at all. Just up against the wall like this with 'is arms up and they was kicking 'im.'[12]

Problems of studying groups

I have not been a member of most of the groups that will be mentioned. As an outsider my information in most cases comes from other peoples' accounts of what makes a group distinct. Those accounts may have been elicited from what Labov[13] terms 'lames', i.e. willing informants who are not fully within the group they purport to be informing about. As an outsider there are always to a greater or lesser extent aspects of the group's way of life that remain hidden. Potentially, by living with the group, more extensive insights may be gleaned about their way of life, but, on the other hand, the participant observer may well eventually give just as an inadequate account of the group's way of life as a newspaper that headlines its story 'all is revealed'. The

87

difficulties of collecting experience and meanings are well revealed in the following extract:

'Whenever I thought I was really "hip", that I really "knew what was happening", something would occur that brought home the extent of my ignorance. For example, on the very last night of my first summer's field work I mistook a challenge to fight for a friendly warning. A Vice Lord said to me, "Hey man, you better walk light!" Because a gang fight had taken place a few hours earlier, and because I had "walk light" used in previous contexts as a friendly warning, I completely misunderstood and responded most inappropriately, "Yeah, I'm hip." Actually, I could not have been more unhip, for "You walk light", or "You better walk light", is usually a challenge to fight, while simply "Walk light", is used as a friendly warning. Because of the complete inappropriateness of my response, my would-be protagonist did not know how to proceed. He stood there for a minute, and then walked across the street and attempted to get other Vice Lords to support him in attacking me. Goliath, however, went over and started threatening him and an argument ensued. Finally, after it was apparent that no one would follow him in "jumping on" me, and some would actively oppose him, he left the corner. I did not find out what had taken place until later when I asked Goliath what the argument across the street had been about.'[14]

Affiliation of teenage groups

Group membership provides a chance of temporary identity in the flux of adolescence. Before the notion was developed in the West that children and childhood were fundamentally 'different' from adults and adulthood, children were expected and were trained to be miniature replicas of adults. Children were not seen as being at all distinctive from adults except in terms of size and experience. Some cultures accept this to be so today. Aries[15] contains a fascinating account of what he calls the 'invention' of childhood in the West. Previously children were expected to behave and talk in the adult way. They worked and shared an adult's day. These children were children only in age. They did not have a way of life of their own that was in any way distinct from adults. They did not form groups which intentionally distinguish themselves from the rest of the community. Adult performance was exemplary. In contrast, for most teenagers in Great Britain today, the threads of affiliation involve certain heroes and heroines that are just slightly older than the group, or even the same age, like the Osmonds, Charlie George, George Best, and those of the locale. A list of heroes and heroines becomes quickly irrelevant because changing the object of adulation is a characteristic method to retain group identity and particular membership.[16] However, as within most groups, individuals have other affiliations, for instance, admiration of war heroes like Winston Churchill, reflecting the admiration of their parents. But when he is with his peers, the teenager has a distinct set of heroes and experiences embodying a particular lexis.

I have found it difficult to find adequate categories for teenage groups. Using the set of categories mentioned earlier:

Geographical proximity or locale	Street gangs
Recreational pursuits	Music fans, scouts, greasers, Hell's Angels
Social class	Skinheads, teds, mods, rockers, hippies, beats
Religious loyalty	Catholic versus Protestant Celtic versus Rangers Royalist versus Republicans Hare Krishna Temple
Age	Teenie bopper, weenie bopper
Sex	Some street gangs
Common heroes, ideology	CND, army cadet force, some students in 68–69, hips, beats, flower people, Hell's Angels

This is not satisfactory, nor are Yablonsky's[17] categories of social, delinquent and violent groups. Here you get something like:

Social	Street gangs, scouts, music fans, greasers, army cadets, flower people?, flower power?, beats?, teds?, skinheads?, hippies?
Delinquent	Hippies?, beats?, army cadets?, CND?, students in 68–69?, skinheads?, teds?, mods?, rockers?, Hell's Angels?, Black Panthers?, etc. etc.
Violent	Loyalist and Republican groups, Hell's Angels, skinheads?

The distinction between social and violent groups seems clear,

89

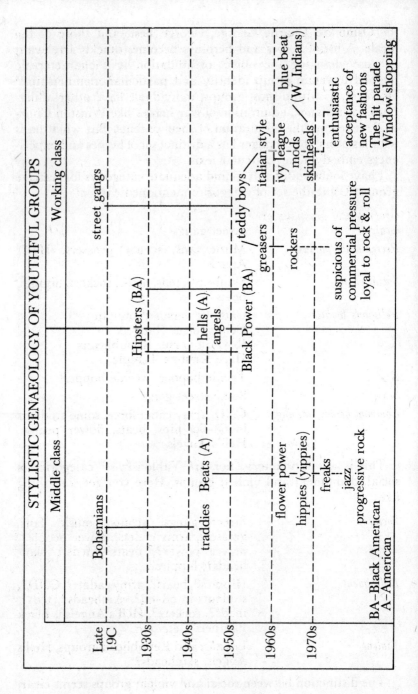

STYLISTIC GENAEOLOGY OF YOUTHFUL GROUPS

Middle class | Working class

Late 19C — Bohemians

1930s — traddies — street gangs

1940s — Beats (A) — Hipsters (BA) — hells (A) angels

1950s — Black Power (BA) — teddy boys

1960s — flower power — greasers — italian style — ivy league — mods — skinheads — blue beat (W. Indians)
hippies (yippies) — rockers — suspicious of commercial pressure — loyal to rock & roll — enthusiastic acceptance of new fashions — The hit parade — Window shopping

1970s — freaks — jazz — progressive rock

BA – Black American
A – American

90

but between these two and delinquent it is hazy. Doubt about where to place particular groups seems to relate to the degree of threat to the established social order that the author feels is evident. Yablonsky does not consider that the violent gang has the characteristics of a group. In his terms it is a 'near group', not a mob or crowd, yet not a 'normal' group.

Teenage groups might be more adequately represented to outsiders if these aspects were considered:

1. The collections of middle-class and working-class values that underlie the actions of the respective teenage groups.
2. The argots which are used to express the experiences of group members.

For example, the skinheads share many features in common with the street gangs of Chicago in the 1930s, as described by W. H. Whyte.[18] The skinheads[19] express in a particularly boisterous way the values of urban working-class. Cohen (op. cit.) specifically presents nine cases of middle-class values, which are rejected by the working-class child. These include the following notions:

(1) Ambition is a virtue, (2) an emphasis on the middle-class ethic of responsibility, (3) a high value on the cultivation of skills and tangible achievement, (4) postponement of immediate satisfactions and self-indulgence in the interest of achieving long-term goals, (5) rationality in the sense of forethought, planning, and budgetting of time, (6) the rational cultivation of manners, courtesy, personality, (7) the need to control physical aggression and violence, (8) the need for wholesome recreation, and (9) the respect for property and its proper care.

If we use the schema on page 90, then the argots may be considered as variations on middle-class and working-class vernacular. The extent to which unique features are present in an argot would be related to the extent that the group has esoteric experiences which embody group meanings. If we set down these distinctive experiences that are shared by real members of the group, then the argots will be within their original contexts. That is, the argots will not be torn from the context and then have meanings assigned to them by the media:

'Contrary to the popular yet erroneous images created by the West Side Story and other glamorized "fictional" versions of violent gang activity, the sociopathic gang youth maintains a type of

91

homosexual relationship system in the gang that reflects his personality. The youth who tends more towards a compassionate female relationship is generally a more marginal violent-gang member. The most sociopathic core gang members will ridicule the youth who attempts to relate to a girl on a human level beyond a simple "sexual trick" or as an object for exploitation.'[20]

Working-class groups are understood, often protected by, and protective to, their families. Their argot shares much of the lexis from the vernacular of working-class city adults. A bit of 'bovver', for instance, with a 'chiv' (an open razor) is not new vocabulary, but has been in the vernacular of East End working-class people for many years. The media have merely made more widely public the way of life of previously 'invisible' groups (e.g. in such television programmes as *Till Death us do Part*). Although the working-class teenage groups are often in active opposition to middle-class values, the middle-class teenage groups often have only the values of their parents to oppose.

It is when a member, or the whole of the group, fails at something that is expressive of group identity that the covert values of the group are expressed overtly, frequently in talk and other actions. So, although values cannot be directly observed, they can be inferred and perhaps substantiated through interview with the members.

Kenneth Stoddart describes his investigations into the usage of the term 'pinched' in a heroin-using community:

'In the course of a conversation with Hughie I queried him regarding the whereabouts of Harry, a heroin user I'd met in the cafe. Hughie told me he'd "been pinched". I asked Hughie what he'd been arrested for and he replied, "For junk, whad did ya think?"

'Hughie's remarks suppose that the character of Harry's arrest is determinable from the pronouncement "he's been pinched". I concluded that for Hughie when one is pinched, one is arrested for the possession of narcotics.

'However, the sense of the term remained to be determined— as I discovered. Supposing now that "pinched" referred to an arrest for possession of narcotics I thought that it might be warrantable to inquire into the nature of such an arrest: instead of asking for what one was pinched, I could ask how one was pinched. The following field-note displays the posing of that question:

'Earlier in the evening I'd heard that John had been arrested for possession of narcotics. I mentioned this to Robbie: "I hear

92

John's been pinched." "Yeah, so I hear", she said. I asked, "How did it happen?" and Robbie replied: "What the fuck do you mean, how did it happen? The same way they all happen, I guess."

'During the course of a conversation Hughie asked me if I'd been to the Family Cafe recently. I replied that I had and he asked "Anybody been pinched?" Earlier in the week I'd heard that Lynn, a lesbian of our mutual acquaintance, had been arrested for vagrancy. I thus replied, "I heard Lynn was". Hughie expressed some surprise and said: "Jeez, I didn't know she was using". I told him what she'd been arrested for and he said, "Oh, I meant for junk".'[21]

Expressions of disappointment or failure indicate what the group holds to be of worth or praise. So 'all screwed up' (value: to be at peace with the world), 'he ratted', 'split on me' (value: do not tell others, especially police or others in authority about the group or members of the group), 'to lose rep(utation)' (value: defend your status), 'to be turfed out' (value: defend your territory), 'freak out' (value: try to keep self-control in order to appreciate the effects of LSD. [Speculatively, 'freaked out' may have some connotation with the Todd Browning film of the thirties, *Freaks*. Interestingly, in the later sixties, Jesus Phreaks appeared, but, seemingly to distinguish (in print at least) 'freaked out' (LSD effects) from the effects of divine inspiration, 'freak' became 'phreak' so Jesus Phreaks.] As an example of a very concise expression of values in argot, let us look at 'turn on, tune in, drop out' in which, in a very few words, a whole life style and its values is portrayed. The suggestion is that one should 'turn on' and take some sort of soft drugs, 'tune in' or become attuned to what one's contemporaries are doing by (particularly) not wanting to fight in Vietnam, and 'drop out' of the rat-race and the society which made the Vietnam policy possible.

The relatively simple term 'language' in the title of this essay contains a number of reference terms and factors which have had to be unpacked. First of all, language is linked inextricably with, and some would say opens out of, the society in which it occurs. Secondly, a system of values is expressed by language and is made possible by language, and when that system of values needs to be kept secret as in the case of some teenage groups, then language is again used to undertake that secrecy. But language is itself too broad a concept to be used with sufficient delicacy, as we have found, and so further terms were needed to explain some of the

93

linguistic phenomena of teenage groups. Thus having dealt with a part of the title of the essay, we now turn and look at the other main aspect, namely the types of particular teenage groups.

Some teenage groups

TEDDY BOYS

Duration circa 1953–58, with a few enclaves, e.g. Elephant and Castle, Mile End, Norwich, still existing in 1974.

Emblems
Dress
Men: Edwardian draped single-breasted jackets, velvet collars, with tight trousers (drainpipes), thick crepe-soled shoes (Jesus creepers), bright coloured socks, shirts with cut-away collars and bootlace or very narrow ties.
Girls: pen line two-piece, extremely tight tapering skirt called the 'hobble', stiletto-heeled shoes.

Hairstyle
Men: Tony Curtis or District Attorney, abbreviation DA, redubbed 'duck's arse', heavily greased. Frequent public self-grooming with comb.
Girls: bouffant.

Characteristic Experience
It should be kept in mind that the Teds were the first identifiable distinct group of teenagers with a life style of their own (although the actual dress was said to have been recreated amongst young city gentlemen). The Teddy Boys coincided with increased earnings for young people, national service, the end of rationing, and rock 'n' roll. Jeff Nuttall[22] has written that the Teddy Boys celebrated with violence. When searched by police they were often found, according to news reports, to be carrying bicycle chains, flick knives and various other potentially dangerous weapons. An interesting period of their existence, one that brought them into the public eye, concerns their response to the film *Blackboard Jungle*. This was about a school in the city of New York and the teachers' difficulties in retaining control. The music for the film was played by Bill Haley and his Comets, and it was the Teddy Boys response to the music that amazed and frightened adults. The film had been preceded by reports of wild violent dancing

94

and destruction of cinemas in the United States. When the film was shown in Great Britain police were always at the ready to intervene should the response become too boisterous. Often it did. There were fights, seats were slit and destroyed and people were injured, so the police had to move in.

Values

Although the mass media presented the Teddy Boys as uncontrollable animals, if their group is studied, their underlying values are not markedly different from those of the urban working classes. For instance, they frequently lived at home with their parents, worked in semi-skilled jobs, or as apprentices, attended organized clubs and pubs, disliked but feared the police, and acknowledged dating, engagements, and accepted females into the group. If the relationship between distinctive values and distinctive argot is useful, then the Teddy Boys, as a group, illustrate the non-distinctiveness of their values from the other adults in the community by not having a distinctive argot, only a limited lexis to describe their appearance, viz. beetle crushers, Jesus creepers, chivs. Their enjoyment of rock 'n' roll—Haley, Little Richard, Jerry Lee Lewis, early Elvis, was expressive of their energetic masculine style. The established popular music of the time—Vera Lynn, Winifred Atwell, Dickie Valentine, Eve Boswell, was incapable of being related to by the Teds and many other young people.

THE TRADDIES (mouldy figs)

A good description of the Traddies can be found in Humphrey Lyttleton's *Second Chorus*[23] in which the group is seen by an adult, who, as he led a jazz band, came into daily contact with teenagers who centred much of their life and later their values around the traditional jazz revival of the Fifties. The traditional jazz revival was an Anglo-American phenomenon; professional and amateur musicologists discovered the origins of jazz in the persons of ageing former musicians like Bunk Johnson whose careers had suffered a decline in the intervening years. The revival was an appeal to an earlier 'golden age'—in this case the music of the twenties, or more exactly the music of certain jazz bands of the twenties in certain cities in America.

Whereas the Teds urged to free themselves from the cloying, traditional authority of parents, teachers and police, the traddies were far more sedate. Music recovered from the past provided

95

a focus for the group. The values of the musicologist's genuineness (compared to 'pseudo') non-commercialism, sincerity, became those of the music's followers. In appearance, trads often were dishevelled, in jeans, sandals (all the year round), loose long sweaters; an exaggeration of the sort of thing middle-class parents might wear on holiday (apart from the jeans). Whereas the Teds had a style which incorporated the latest in fashion and were thus 'commercial', the trad's attire was home-spun and functional. Unlike the Teds, trad girls often wore similar clothes to the men. The girls' similar appearance reflected their equal rights in mating and dating, and, unlike the Teds, traditional institutions like couples and engagements were somewhat disdained. The girls often dressed in the style of the singer Juliette Greco and this, I think, reflects the other main source of values of the traddies—French existentialism represented by Jean Paul Sartre and Simone de Beauvoir.

Whereas the Teds enjoyed displaying themselves in public in pubs and clubs and on the streets, the traddies preferred more private places—coffee bars and cellar jazz clubs. The contrasting behaviour of the traddies and Teds derives from their middle-class and working-class values. Many of the trads were in line for professional careers—teachers, painters, poets. They looked back to the Bohemian tradition in Britain and also incorporated the Zen Buddhist-influenced philosophy of their American contemporaries, the Beats.

The Argot

A 'pseudo' is one who is not truly a member of the group, especially one who pretends to be unconcerned about commercialism, but the rest of the group really knows he is. 'Gone commercial'—especially about a musician who has started to play only if paid, who begins to dress respectably, and who tries to appeal to a wider audience. Also, about a 'traddy' who seems to be influenced by advertising and other commercial interests. 'Sincere', not in it for profit, only the experience. 'Authentic'—the real thing, mainly applied to primitive musicianship (possession of excessive technique was identified with commercialism). 'Existential', trying to experience anything and everybody that happened to come along.

The Campaign for Nuclear Disarmament found a lot of support amongst the traddies. Often processions would be led by a jazz band. Political awareness amongst the traddies may be contrasted to the absence of any political interest amongst the Teds. It seems to me that the collection of values, although from disparate sources, were complementary to each other, existentialism, Zen, jive talk, CND. The threat of nuclear annihilation with its associated arms race, testing programmes, fall-out shelters, etc. generated a clear alternative set of values like universal brotherhood, peace, help for poor nations, taking a stand against warmongers, civil disobedience at strategic sites, revealing secret official plans, taking the risk of going to jail. So, although the traddies' basic values were middle-class there were strong embellishments from other sources which reflected in the argot which was distinct from the middle-class vernacular of the time. Although the traddies were the first distinct teenage group influenced by political ideas that were often contrary to those of their parents, in addition to the ideological influences, the trads were the first teenage group to use marijuana (tea, pot, muggles, Mary Jane, and so on). Use of marijuana was complementary to many of the ideas expressed in jazz and blues songs in the twenties and thirties.[24]

HIPPIES

Turn on, tune in, freak (drop out). The hippies evolved from the American middle-class beats. Long hair was the initial emblem of membership. Attempting to describe the other initiation component, the LSD experience, spawned a new lexis whose meanings could only be appreciated by those who shared the feelings and imagery which LSD provided. Although 'freak out' and 'I'm flying' later became part of a more public vocabulary, many of the images remained incomprehensible and meaningless to outsiders. (The hippies' understanding of the song 'Lucy in the Sky with Diamonds' is somewhat different to that of the outsider!) A general point about argot can be made here, that is that as with 'jitterbug', 'rave', 'swinging' and so on, the original meaning of these items as denoters of particular experiences become lost through their 'literal' interpretation engendered through advertising and assimilated as 'with it' by the vernacular.

The hippies, like the trads and beats, are in revolt against the materialist culture and, like the beats, they were concerned with love, nature, and brotherhood. Although initially, in their 'flower power' stage, the hippies loved everyone, including the policemen (later 'fuzz' and 'pigs') and other people in authority, outsiders were soon perjoratively termed 'straight' just as 'squares' were outsiders for hippies and beats, and 'citizens' for Hell's Angels. Like the beats, many of the hippies willingly accepted regular financial support from parents. However, some hippies decided to become agriculturalists and commune dwellers, providing all goods necessary for existence by their own labours. This sub-group, the 'diggers', were often so ignorant and romantic about nature and its beautiful ways that they died of starvation. However, those that survived have shown how successfully it is possible to live without the sophisticated devices of mass production.

The other branch of the hippies were the yippies, who featured heavily at the 1968 Democratic Convention in Chicago and are reported by Norman Mailer:[25]

(Hayden) said that marchers coming to Chicago by the tens of thousands, preferred to be at the Amphitheatre. So the city got ready for a week of disorders its newspapers had advised it to avoid. One can only divine the expression on (Mayor) Daley's face when he read literature like the following—it comes from a throwaway in Lincoln Park, given out on Sunday afternoon, August 25:

YIPPIE

lincoln park

VOTE PIG IN '68

Free Motel
'come sleep with us'

REVOLUTION TOWARDS A FREE SOCIETY
YIPPIE
By A. Yippie

1. An immediate end to the War in Vietnam.
2. Immediate freedom for Huey Newton of the Black Panthers and all other black people.
3. The legalisation of marihuana and all other psychedelic drugs.
4. A prison system based on the concept of rehabilitation rather than punishment.
5. . . . abolition of all laws related to crimes without victims. That is, retention only of laws relating to crimes in which there is an unwilling injured party, i.e. murder, rape, assault.

(followed by 12 other listed items).

. . . Political Pigs, your days are numbered. We are the Second American Revolution. We shall win. Yippie.

The skinheads exhibit in an amplified and frenetic way the values of a section of the working class. An explicit diagram of one skinhead's relationship to other members of society comes from the *Paint House*:

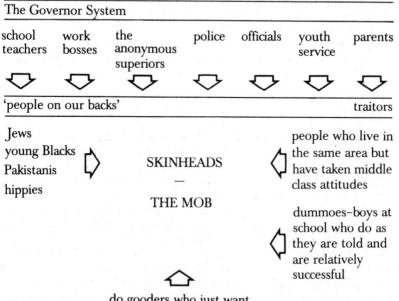

The Governor System

| school teachers | work bosses | the anonymous superiors | police | officials | youth service | parents |

'people on our backs'   traitors

Jews
young Blacks
Pakistanis
hippies

SKINHEADS
—
THE MOB

people who live in the same area but have taken middle class attitudes

dummoes–boys at school who do as they are told and are relatively successful

do gooders who just want to do something for those poor people in the slums

'Everywhere there are fucking bosses, they're always trying to tell you what to do . . . don't matter what you do, where you go. People in authority, the people who tell you what do and make sure you do it. It's the system we live in, the governor system.'

'The governors, they've got authority, they come down on you.'

'Schools, you 'ave to go, doncha? The teachers and the 'eadmaster, they're the authority, ain't they? They're telling you what to do and you're glad to get out and leave 'n that, aren't ya? But work's no different, ya got the bosses there, ain't ya? They think cause you're young, and they pay you and that, that they can treat you how they like and say what they want. They think they're superior.'

'Yeah, there's a whole lot of superiors, ain't there . . . they're like anonymous, ain't they, ya know what I mean. Like when you're in your working clothes, jeans and boots 'n that, then you get on

99

a tube or bus or something, they look at you as if you was dirt, just cause they wear suits and things.'

'Then there's the 'old bill' and courts . . . they're all part of authority. Officials and all kinds of people in uniforms. Anyone with a badge on, traffic wardens and council and that . . . yeah, even the caretaker at the flats; they even 'ave goes at you. Then when you finish at work or at school, you go to the club and the youth leaders are all just a part of it.'

'Your mother and father were the first type of authority. Some parents haven't got any authority when you get older but authority is anyone who's got power over you.'[26]

There is a similarity of values, incorporated in the lexis, between skinheads and delinquent working-class American groups:

'*Trouble:* Concern over "trouble" is a dominant feature of lower-class culture . . . "Trouble" in one of its aspects represents a situation or a kind of behaviour which results in unwelcome or complicating involvement with official authorities or agencies of middle-class society . . . for men, "trouble" frequently involves fighting or sexual adventures while drinking; for women sexual involvement with disadvantageous consequences. Expressed desire to avoid behaviour which violates moral or legal norms is often based less on an explicit commitment to "official" moral or legal standards than on a desire to avoid "getting into trouble", e.g. the complicating consequences of the action.

'*Toughness:* The concept of "toughness" in lower-class culture represents a compound combination of qualities or states. Among its most important components are physical prowess, evidenced both by demonstrated possession of strength and endurance and athletic skill; "masculinity" symbolised by a complex of acts and avoidance (bodily tattooing, absence of sentimentality; non-concern with art, literature; conceptualisation of women as conquest objects, etc.); and bravery in the face of physical threat. The model for the tough guy—hard, fearless, undemonstrative, skilled in physical combat—is represented by the movie gangster of the thirties, the "private eye", and the movie cowboy.

'*Smartness:* "Smartness" . . . involves the capacity to outsmart, outfox, outwit, dupe, "take", "con" another or others, and the concomitant capacity to avoid being outwitted, "taken" or duped oneself. In its essence, smartness involves the capacity to achieve a valued entity—material goods, personal status—through a maximum use of mental agility and a minimum of physical effort.

'*Excitement:* For many lower-class individuals the rhythm of life fluctuates between periods of relatively routine or repetitive

100

activity and sought situations of great emotional stimulation. Many of the most characteristic features of lower-class life are related to the search for excitement or "thrill". Involved here are the widespread use of gambling of all kinds . . . The quest for excitement finds . . . its most vivid expression in the recurrent "night on the town" . . . a patterned set of activities in which alcohol, music, and sexual adventuring are major components.'[27]

The New York gangs described by Yablonsky make finer distinctions—expressed in lexis—for their experience of 'toughness' and 'trouble'.

'One is when we go on a "stomp". That's when three or four guys will jump one, for no reason at all . . . They go down and grab a guy for any reason at all. They'll sometimes beat up a guy on their own team—it doesn't make any difference—they just want to stomp someone.

'Second kind is a "Jap". That's when a group of guys, two guys or three guys, go down to a different club's territory, get in fast, beat up one or two guys, and get out. The thing is not to get caught. They can do that with fists or they go in sometimes with guns, knives, depends on the group they're fighting.

'Third is a "bop". That can be a small group, five, ten, twenty guys from one team, having it out with the same number from a different team. It doesn't make any difference; it doesn't mean that those two teams are actually at war with each other, it's just that it's one of those clashes.

'The fourth is a "rumble". That's when both clubs are getting everybody they can—brother gangs and all—to go out and fight. It's an all-out gang war . . .

'Gangs sometimes say when they're gonna rumble that they'll give you a fair one; that's when one guy from one team will meet another guy from another, and it's supposed to be just between those two guys. Just two guys, nobody else is supposed to butt in.'[28]

The situation in schools

This essay is intended to transmit the message that teenage groups are still basically expressing class values. Dress, hair-style, heroes, and haunts may change along with the labels, but the basic values remain similar. The argot is often concerned with descriptions of dress and with particular experiences of that teenage group. However, drugs and adult ideologies have altered some of the traditional class values and this is reflected in the degree of variation of the argot from the vernacular.

What I have attempted to show is that teenagers have a life outside of school which has its own rules, language and system of values, and that these are enmeshed together. Inevitably such a network of interrelating and interlocking factors spills over into school in the sense that the teenagers who still have to come to school do not, cannot, leave their affiliations (social class, age, group or gang, values etc.) at the school gate to be picked up again at the end of school. Often schools try to make teenagers leave their affiliations at home by the expedient of not allowing teenage 'gear' into schools. But whether the teenage gear is banned or not—and anyway it is only the outward and visible signs of an inward and invisible commitment—teenagers have outside affiliations which they bring into school. In fact the battle that goes on in some schools over teenage gear perhaps highlights the entrenched attitudes that can exist on both sides. Teachers and teenagers see teenage 'culture' as something to be fought over. Teenage gear is one such *causus belli*. Another is the language of teenagers.

Concerning the language of teenagers, teachers see such language as antipathetic: teenage language is 'slovenly' and is full of terms which the adult cannot and is not supposed to understand. It embodies a system of values which teachers may feel threatens their own; it is used against teachers deliberately to exclude them. This could be said to be a view of a teacher dealing daily with teenagers at school. But an examination of the view from the teenagers' point will be of value here. Teenagers feel threatened by the constant pressure exerted on them by adults to conform to adult values, adult language and adult affiliations. Teachers have to realize (and many have) that experiences provided by the school are not the only ones in the life of a teenager. Teachers might also realize that the expression of values in behaviour is not exclusively to do with being a teenager, but also with social class differences.

What I have written about is in a sense historical, but I hope that what I have had to say about teenage groups gives some insights into the meaning of teenage behaviour which have continuity. By concentrating on the language of teenage groups it is possible to see that what the special languages of the groups embody are different sets or systems of values. When these values change, and they are harder to change than organizational structures, then it will be possible to see the new meanings expressed in the new language which will be needed. Thus the continuing interest and usefulness of considering the language of teenage groups.

References

[1]A detailed discussion of some of the problems of categorizing the varieties of language usage is to be found in: Labov W. (1972) 'Some Problems of Linguistic Methodology' in *Language in Society*, Vol. *1*, pp. 97–155, Cambridge University Press.

[2]Song by Peter Townshend of 'The Who', © (1965) Fabulous Music Ltd, London.

[3]Fowler, P. (1972), *Rock File*, ed. C. Gillet, New English Library, London.

[4]Palmer, T. (1971), *The Trials of Oz*, Blond and Briggs, London.

[5]Goodman, Paul (1961) *Growing Up Absurd*, Gollancz, London.

[6]La Fontaine, J. S. (1970), in *Socialisation: the Approach from Social Anthropology*, ed. Mayer, M., Tavistock, London.

[7]In Becker, H. S. (1963), *Outsiders*, Free Press of Glencoe, New York. *See* also Castaneda, C. (1970), *The Teachings of Don Juan*, Penguin, London.

[8]Labov, W. (1966), Appendix B, *The Social Stratification of English in New York City*, PhD Thesis, Centre for Applied Linguistics, Columbia University, N.Y. (Paul Willis at the Centre for Contemporary Cultural Studies, Birmingham University, has recently been collecting recordings of 'authentic' talk.)

[9]Whyte, op. cit.

[10]Patrick, J. (1973), *Glasgow Gang Observed*, Eyre Methuen, London.

[11]Two excellent illustrations of the relationship between social context and argot are: Sykes, G. M. (1958), *The Society of Captives: a Study of a Maximum Security Prison*, especially Chapter Five, Princetown University Press.
Goffman, E. (1962), 'Cooling the Mark Out', in Rose, A. M. (ed.) *Human Behaviour and Social Process*, Routledge & Kegan Paul, London.

[12]Daniel, S. and McGuire, P. (1972), (eds) *The Paint House*, Penguin, London.

[13]Labov, W. (1973), 'The Linguistic Consequences of Being a Lame', in *Language in Society 2*, pp. 81–115, April 1973.

[14]Keiser, R. L. (1970), 'Fieldwork Among the Vice Lords of Chicago', in *Being an Anthropologist*, Spindler, G. (ed.), Holt, Rinehart and Winston Inc., N.Y.

[15]Aries, P. (1974), *Centuries of Childhood*, Jonathan Cape.
[16]*See* Cohen, S. (1972), *Folk Devils and Moral Panics*, McGibbon and Kee, London.
[17]Yablonsky, L. (1970), *The Violent Gang*, Macmillan, N.Y.
[18]Whyte, W. H. (1943), *Street Corner Society*, Chicago University Press, issued in 1969 in Great Britain.
[19]As represented in Daniel & McGuire, op. cit.
[20]Quoted in Yablonsky, op. cit.
[21]Stoddart, K. (1974), 'Pinched: Notes on the Ethnographers Location of Argot' in Turner, R. (ed.) *Ethnomethodology*, Penguin, London.
[22]Nuttall, J. (1968), *Bomb Culture*, MacGibbon and Kee, London.
[23]Lyttleton, H. (1958), *Second Chorus*, MacGibbon and Kee, London. *See* also Melly, G. (1972), *Owning up*, Weidenfeld and Nicolson, London.
[24]*See* for instance Mezzrow, M. (1946), *Really the Blues*, Secker and Warburg, London.
[25]Mailer, N. (1968), *Miami and the Seige of Chicago*, Weidenfeld and Nicolson, London.
[26]Daniel & McGuire, op. cit.
[27]Yablonsky, op. cit.
[28]Yablonsky, op. cit.

Additional literature could include:

Mailer, N. 'The White Negro', an essay in *Advertisements for Myself*, Deutsch, London.
Major, C. (1971), *Black Slang*, Routledge & Kegan Paul, London.
Kerouack, J. (1972), *On the Road*, Andre Deutsch, London.
Roszak, T. (1970), *The Making of a Counter Culture*, Faber and Faber, London.
Labov, W. (1972), 'Rules for ritual insults' in D. Sudnow (ed.) *Studies in Social Interaction*, Free Press, New York.
Wieder, L. *Language and Reality: the case for convict code*, Mouton.
Agar, M. (1973) 'Talking about doing: lexicon and event' in *Language in Society*, *3*, pp. 83–89.
Gosling, R. *Sum Total*, Faber & Faber, London.
McInnes, C. *Absolute Beginners*, MacGibbon and Kee, London.
Salinger, J. D. *Catcher in the Rye*, Penguin.
Steel, R. 'Letter from Oakland—The Panthers', *N.Y. Review of Books*, 11 September 1969.

Relevant films

TRAD/TEDS: *Mama Don't Allow*
HELL'S ANGELS: *The Wild Ones*
Scorpio Rising
GREASERS: *The Leather Boys*
BEATS: *Pull My Daisy*
HIPPIES: *Easy Rider*
Getting Straight
Alice's Restaurant
MODS: *Two Left Feet* (1963)

MISCELLANEOUS:

Medium Cool, Directed by H. Waxler. 1968.
Film about the Chicago Convention, 1968.
Rebel Without a Cause
Smashing Time
The Knack
Blow-Up
Taking Off
How We Were
Blackboard Jungle
Lonely Boy (documentary about the early pop star
Paul Anka)

Acknowledgements

My thanks for their constructive comments to:
Stuart Hall, Paul Willis, Rob Walker, Liz Saunders and Deirdre Burton.

5 Talk about pop

RAMSEY W. RUTHERFORD

Foreword

The two extracts which follow exemplify teenage talk about pop as recorded in a girls' school in the north of England. The extracts are meant not only to illustrate the topic 'pop', but also to illustrate the way in which pop is talked about. The way that these children have of talking about pop may be revealed by underlining each occurrence of the word 'just' as you read through the extracts, and then by taking a second run-through to note the context of each occurrence. Lastly I ask you to seek a gloss or a 'translation' of what the word means in each case. In the second extract, can I ask you particularly to look at sentence length and sentence simplicity? Having done so, can you believe that the same girls could produce much more subtle and coherent language on another topic, for example a topic that we in the Child Language Survey have called 'Relationships—Human, with Adults'? (See Example 6, on p. 114.)

EXTRACT ONE

(X is me, the adult interviewer; the other speakers are three girls aged 13–15 years):

X. Well, wha ... what's so good about him? You know, what
    ma ... what picks him out as being better than anybody
    else?
    Oh. (laugh)
    (laugh)
    His voice ...
    Just ... just different ...
    Well, not just his voice ...
    From everybody else. (laugh)
    But himself. (laugh)
    Him ... just him.

X. What about himself?
Well, just ... (laugh)
Erm ...
So nice, you know ...
His looks, his nature, everything.
X. Do you know him?
Well ...
No.
You listen to interviews ...
But y ... y ... (laugh)
You just get to know him ...
And things ...
Seeing him on television and things and ...
Yeah.
Seeing interviews and things of him, you just get to know
his character and everything.
X. What kind of character? .
Oh, he's very generous ...
And kind ...
Mm.
And kind and ... you know.
Yeah.

EXTRACT TWO

X. There are people who are w ... who don't like him?
Yeah, you either ...
Oh, yes ...
Like him or hate him.
Quite a few actually.
Most, erm, younger people like him, but you know, they
don't really like (laugh) him, you know, just sort of 'cos
everyone likes him at that age. But not so many people at
our age like him now, do they?
Mm ... well, quite a ...
Well, no ...
Few do, I suppose, but ... well, not in our class anyway.
N ... no ....
M ...
Not many, really.
No, not many.
It's really the class below and downwards.
Mm.
They don't really like him like we do. (laugh)
(laughter)
X. Well, have they moved on to somebody else?
Yes.

X. The people in your class.
Well ...
X. Have they got more ...
I don't know ... I don't think ...
X. Mature tastes than you have?
Nooo, it's ...
(laughter)
It's just that they have a new one, really.
Well, I suppose they did, but, you know ...
(unintelligible)
You see, he hasn't been all that popular for long, has he?
No.
They probably ...
A few years only.
Just don't like that sort of song, so they have no interest in
the person perhaps.
X. Yes. What sort of song do you think they like? The other
people in your class?
(laugh)
Don't know. The same as we like, but not the Osmonds.
(laugh)
'Cos you know, there's the Sweet and all sorts of things, you
know. Just pop music. (laugh)

My object in this foreword has been to allow you, the reader, to
focus on my theme in such a way that you are perfectly well-quali-
fied to quarrel with my exposition as it goes along. Although some
remarks about the occurrences of the word 'just' in the two extracts
can be found in section two under the heading of 'Unanalysability', it as well to make a preliminary examination of my use
of the term 'unanalysability' because most of what I have to say
centres around the concept.

A WORKING DEFINITION OF 'UNANALYSABILITY'

It may be helpful as a preliminary to define the two kinds of meaning I refer to when I use this term, a term which I know of no
one else using (though it is similar perhaps to Stoddart's use of
the term 'opaque' in referring to drug users' terminology). The
two kinds of meaning I refer to are:

a. Language which is INEXPLICIT, VAGUE in reference,
maddeningly REPETITIVE, ELLIPTICAL in style
STEREOTYPED in vocabulary, deathly UNORIGINAL

in syntax, and where word-play would be anathema (I exaggerate for effect).

Example 1 : 'His voice ... just ... just different ...'
Gloss: You'd never believe how utterly.

b. Language which refers to activities, opinions, feelings and wishes which adolescents wish to *conceal* from parents, *share* with their peer-group members, and is *expressed* in the type of language referred to above.
Example 2 : 'Oh, he's just ... erm ... so nice, you know ... His looks, his nature, *everything.*'

The label is rather like a mixture of three things:

1. A racing motorist's *jargon*—language private to a group of enthusiasts freely intended to share that enthusiasm or interest.
2. A drug addicts' or thieves' *argot*—secret language of a group needing to conceal information from those in authority.
3. A schoolboys' or convicts' *code*—don't help the beaks/warders.

In other words, 'unanalysability' is a remarkably effective way of keeping *cave* by an apparently shabby device.

1 Introduction

Children extend their 'world' outside the home and school, beyond their physical environment, through the senses to do with language. They hear about things that they, like adults, can rarely verify for themselves. They build up knowledge of the world outside by acquiring limited descriptions and explanations, and in doing so they usually pick up attitudes to that which is being described according to the dependency that they have on the group that they wish to belong to. At an earlier age, the child is dependent most probably on his or her mother; later it is more likely to be a selected member of the peer group. For many adolescents this means a split allegiance, reflected in language. It will be argued here that the nature of the split allegiance is best seen in the way that the adolescents talk about *certain* topics (but by no means all topics) in their conversations. 'Talking-about-pop singers' is a good example. You will have seen the two extracts contained in the Foreword. The extracts were taken from a longer discussion which was dominated by talk about the singer Donnie Osmond. The speakers were three girls, aged 13.10 years, 13.9

years and 15 exactly. I was the other speaker designated mysteriously as X. The provenance of the recording is described in section six, and the bibliographical details can be found under 'BAC 14' at the end.

When we at the Child Language Survey in Leeds and then York indexed and classified the topics of conversation in the transcripts of our tapes of fifteen-year-old children (Rutherford, Freeth & Mercer 1969), we found that we needed a third general area of classification which we could only classify as the 'Philosophical' domain. That is, topics which the children talked about without immediate personal experience or knowledge—facts or opinions usually derived from television. 'Domestic' and 'Educational' were the other domains that we inherited from our predecessor Richard Handscombe's index of slightly younger children. But with the older children and adolescents that we recorded, we found more and more topics occurring that we simply could not relate to the children's immediate environment of school and home. For example, the most exotic hobbies of the younger children could be accommodated under our rubric 'Interests—Domestic', and trouble with a teacher under 'Relationships with adults—Educational'. But the topic 'Life after Death' that we recorded did not relate to a school lesson or Sunday school, but to an apparently absorbing television programme, which at least one group of Leeds grammar school boys discussed at length with interest. Their experience of death was negligible, but their grasp of acceptable attitudes towards death seemed very adult, though parrotted. I was reminded of the kind of response which always appeals to the audience on seeing and hearing, a few years ago on the television, the responses of Harold Williamson's young interviewees: a cute mirroring of adult views at an age when they can hardly know the true significance of what they are talking about. This is in fact a process which goes on all the time in children's language development, the picking up of 'language models' which are later adjusted according perhaps to life experience.

It is usual for mother-tongue English teachers to try to draw on personally-felt individual impressions in creative work. But it is a fact that they are often disappointed by the conventional models and images produced by their pupils, and rather less often heartened by examples of personal perceptions. I argue here that both kinds are important in development—conventional models *and* personal perceptions, and that for the purposes of this essay I shall be looking at an example of the 'model'—the 'pop' model.

I hold here that the function of such models is essentially *impersonal* (i.e. is a general peer group model to which an adolescent adheres as a member of that group, not as an individual), and may be necessarily so. I label adolescent concepts of this kind 'unanalysable'.

The way in which adolescents speak about pop gives rise to the complaint that they speak another language (section three), while in fact they use another 'logic' (section four), related to their subculture (section five). The topic 'pop' occurring in the adolescent cultural system is 'conversationally related', by which I mean that their system of beliefs and attitudes can be seen through the medium of their conversations. The kernel of the story is section six where the 'pop' model is discussed in the context of the Survey's collection of taped conversations of adolescent interests. The general structure of pop panegyrics in conversations is sketched, thus forming a suggested *preliminary* to the detailed syntactic analysis which so often occurs in the studies of child language without the preliminaries being undertaken.

But no detailed quantitative approach is actually taken up here, though work of this kind is available in several of the Survey's published papers. I have reflected in this essay my recently strengthening belief that we gained more than we thought in the Survey from the actual process of recording and transcribing the conversations and from talking with the children before and after the recordings about their feelings towards them. Also important were discussions with all my colleagues of things which came to our notice as part of our everyday office routine, when we often collectively checked what the children said against our own intuitions and memories of childhood. Since our group essentially remained constant throughout our work it became part of our lives to discuss in this manner, and we never felt the need for formal seminars. This essay reflects some of this more speculative part of our work, which leavened the routine typical of projects concerned with large amounts of data.

2 The notion of 'unanalysability'

A common complaint made about their teenage offspring by adults is that they speak an entirely different language. They don't, quite simply, in any linguistic terms, but it is true to say that adults notice differences in the ways of speaking which irritate them: bits of language in other words, not the whole language.

relating to certain values which most adults do not rate very highly. This more social interpretation of what seems to me to be going on I discuss later, but for the moment I shall keep more closely to the questions of language proper.

These small differences in language which are noticed mean that the speaker who produced them is seen as not belonging to the same 'group' as we, the 'hearers' or 'audience'. It means that the speakers are seen as belonging to another group, perhaps on the basis of a single feature, barely noticeable until pointed out. This feature may be a whiff of intonation in a Welsh or Geordie speaker, plus perhaps a vowel quality which does not quite fit into the standard English system. A Glaswegian to most English people is often seen as producing almost everything differently. These features are indexical in that they indicate that a speaker belongs to a particularly recognizable group, whether of speakers of a particular dialect, or of teenagers, or of girls as opposed to boys.

The speaker is likely to share the overt values of the group he or she belongs to (reference group), so that *values* are indexical as well as bits of language. For example, if one person states publicly and loudly that Glasgow Celtic is the best team on earth, or that Donnie Osmond is the greatest, then that person is likely to be a male teenage resident of Glasgow very likely of catholic parentage or belonging to a group of predominantly catholic boys. He belongs, or indicates that he belongs, to four different reference groups, with more-or-less overlapping values. The problem comes when loyalties are strained to one of these groups, and, as we will see, this is often a problem for a teenager if his family reference group has different values from his other reference groups, for example his peer group. I chose the two extracts because they seemed to me to be indexical of the way teenagers talk about pop, and the set of values that the peer group attributes to pop. The feature that seems to highlight this difference is that of unanalysability.

But before going further, can we look at our modest piece of homework on the word 'just', which seems to me to be used as a typical-enough feature of the inexplicit way teenagers choose to talk about pop. The first point is that the word occurs simply too often in passage one to be standard usage. Secondly, it stands in place of the superlative by implication (i.e. X is the *different* detergent = the best detergent or pop singer = just the best). The word is one of that class of adverbs called these days *intensifiers*, words which draw attention to a quality an object or a person

112

has, made even more powerful by also being a *specifier* (in Green-baum's schema), which means pointing out even more particularly the uniqueness of the quality which an object or person possesses. In our extracts its power is sadly weakened by having to 'intensify' such adjectives as 'nice', or such un-unique subjects as 'him'.

How about the sentences in our extracts? Will anyone quarrel with the label simple? Or largely unconnected? If clauses or sentences are unconnected, then little argumentation is going on, usually. The obvious is being implied. So is it here. Before we leave the point, are we going to predict whether these girls can produce more complex utterances about another topic? I leave the question for the moment. Now we can look at 'unanalysability' from a more common-sense or lay point of view (though there is a certain amount of 'common' sense about linguistics too).

I find that there is virtually nothing you can say about adolescent remarks like:

Example 3: "Well, not just his voice ... but himself."
or
Example 4: "Well, just ... (laugh) him."
or
Example 5: "You just get to know him ... *and things.*"

I therefore label such remarks as unanalysable. Such remarks are, though, important, because they are intended to prevent adult onlookers from explicitly understanding the feeling expressed, and to *allow* peer group members to share in it. This kind of language (and the adolescent attitudes it expresses) is what this essay is about. If you want to sound like a teenager talking about pop you must normally use this kind of language, however intelligent you are, because the *topic* and *situations* are appropriate to this style being used.

What this essay is *not* about is analytical, explicit, adult language influenced by books and the Holy Grail of spoken prose: that version of spoken English where no-one makes mistakes or pauses by mistake. If you want to talk like any other teenager talking about pop, then you must *not* speak in this analysed and analytical manner. However, when the topic changes, the appropriate style very often changes too. For an example of this, let us look at the same girls talking about an incident revealing their relationship to a nun. In the following example, one speaker talks about Sister D. turning them out of the chemistry laboratory where they claim to have been putting gas taps off (and not on).

Example 6:
'Everybody else had gone, apart from Susan and I. And we were really enjoying ourselves playing Donnie records. She came in and it was only about quarter past or ten past.
In fact it was only about eight o'clock and, er, she said, "Everybody else has gone now—come along, clear up."
And we said, "Well, you know, we didn't have to go to bed until half past, can't we stay and listen to Donnie?"
And she said, "No, I'm not waiting here for you two."
And we said, "Well please sister, you know we're meant to have this free time."
She's meant to look after us then, isn't she?
Yeah.
Just because some people have gone it doesn't mean that we have to go. So anyway ... she made us come up.
And I ... and you know, we kept saying things like, "And Donnie was singing 'It's Hard to Say Goodbye'."
And we were saying, "Yes, it is hard to say goodbye to a good record, isn't it?" (laugh).'

There is very little wrong with this as a piece of effective-enough ordered speaking, all perfectly explicit and analysed, and the anecdote works quite well, even though it is explicitly expressed, because the analytic style is appropriate to the topic. The idea that adolescents (of the age specified) might talk about things that their parents do not know about (do not realize interests or obsesses them) in a covert, indirect or secretive way is easy to understand but difficult for many parents to accept.

Of course, parents accept and often encourage their children to go off with other children to play, but it often comes as an uncomfortable shock to realize that such play involves fantasy which would wither on being seen by the common sense of the parent ('Ever let the Fancy roam, Pleasure never is at home'). The life of adolescents is meant to be secretive otherwise it would not exist, and this secretiveness is a necessary mechanism to allow the child to grow up, which means grow away from the parent. It must not be forgotten that it is convenient for the parent that this should happen, since few would want their children to be entirely dependent upon them for all their days.

The secret nature of the life of adolescents is reflected in their language. They need a linguistic way to shield their interests from adults if these interests hold the slightest element of fantasy. This means that adolescents refer to their objects of fantasy in such a way that members of their peer group understand and their parents don't (necessarily). They refer, then, to concepts which *must* not be analysed or explained in adults' common sense terms, but fit, if you like, adolescents' logic—an interim model of common sense logic which changes with age. In another year or so, other objects of fantasy and interest dominate, a year earlier and the topic is almost unthinkable. It will be argued later that the sample discussion of Donnie Osmond is unanalysed and typical in that he could be replaced in innumerable other conversations about any other pop star. If technical details of the music and the voice were discussed analytically the element of shared fantasy would disappear, and hence the notion of 'unanalysability' in adolescents' conversation applies to certain topics only of adolescent interest.

We may now speculate further about the reasons the girls aged 13–15 might have for not analysing their admiration for favourite pop singers:

a. Music in association with such a 'sex object' forms a model, as it were, of most unfulfilled adolescent desires shared preferably only with persons 'sensed' to have similar feelings, and not shared with those known or sensed not to have such feelings. This includes other adolescents of the same age or group, and excludes most adults.

b. Since such feelings about sex are confidential, then those feelings associated with sex objects like pop stars are also confidential.

c. Analysing anything is a rational process which most people have to learn to do, and is particularly difficult to do when it has to do with something you do not want to analyse, because, as in this case the idea is to participate in such feelings not analyse them.

d. Pop stars appealing to this age group are often themselves very young and may be relatively lacking in strong personality characteristics.

One can look at the language produced on such occasions as adolescents talking in an unanalysed way about pop stars from the point of view of the linguistic concepts of audience and style. It may be said that style in conversation needs to be defined negatively. You know if you are being addressed as the wrong kind of 'audience': as someone lower in status than you feel entitled to believe you really are, for example. This may be revealed to you simply by use of an over-intimate manner of speaking on too-short acquaintance. You believe you have been inappropriately 'placed' by your interlocutor according to the way you have been talked to, by the 'style' of his discourse.

How does this idea of style and audience help us in treating unanalysed topics of conversation? Basically, as an adult, you are eavesdropping on a bit of conversation not intended for you even though you may be actually present in the flesh at the scene of the conversation, and perhaps even provide the topic. The unanalysed manner of developing the topic signals the intended audience—other interested members of the peer group (not adults, though their right to be present may only rarely be challenged). It is, nevertheless, always puzzling to witness bits of conversation which go on as though you were not present, not couched in terms intended to appeal to adult logic. You are, as it were, an uncomfortably inappropriate audience, the wrong addressee.

3 The Secret Language is the 'Secretive' Culture

A surprising number of sophisticated mothers complain that their young adolescent children speak 'a completely different language'. Fathers rarely complain about this, it seems. Their wives have acted as interpreters since their children began to utter sequences (see Snow's essay), and their wives' responsibilities for the job continues into their children's adolescence. But then the job of interpretation has changed in perhaps the most puzzling way possible—translating a partially alien cultural system.

Translating short utterances relating to the baby's immediate needs is difficult, but trial and error plus shrewd guessing leads to an interim understanding of his language system at a given time. The baby refers mostly to the immediate world of himself and his mother, and in a related way beyond. His feelings too are usually catered for in the same way by what Broadbent calls the 'guess-and-check method': the basic methodology of research in physics and other hypothesized finite systems. This methodology is not entirely adequate for research into social systems, and quite inadequate for translating alien cultures. One has to invoke the concept of perceptual constancy in psychology to account for the way in which speakers of a language assume, against much contrary evidence, that one language means one culture. It is most convenient for all concerned to think so. So it can be seen that it is inconvenient to think that the adolescent whose language needs have earlier been so completely serviced by the mother, should so willingly participate in an alien and secretive sub-culture, that of his peer group. 'Pop' is one of the totems of this sub-culture, which is why it is discussed here.

This sub-culture is necessarily partially secretive or evasive for reasons discussed in section two under the rubric of 'unanalys-ability'. It is a sub-culture because it caters for only a part of the adolescents' social needs, the 'mother' culture serving for the rest. Neither culture is the more important; both are necessary. In order that a secretive culture shall remain so it is necessary to refer to it evasively without explaining it. If it is largely an entrance ticket to group feeling of outward-seeking emotional needs then it is intrinsically unanalysed. There is no need to analyse it if you are a group member. An adult is not a group member and is impatient of the rules prohibiting analysis and seeks ready-made explanations constructed out of adult logic. (See next section.)

So the different language of which parents complain is different not because the basic syntactic 'rules' are different, but because the language refers to unanalysed concepts in an alien but related sub-culture which has its own set of totems. An adolescent going through a sullen silent stage may be suffering a particularly painful form of the bi-culturism which afflicts exiles. How can one talk about totems in a way that will appeal to adult logic? In passing, it seemed to me that girls of the age this essay is about seem more able than boys to find acceptable evasive linguistic formulas.

If we compare adolescent idols with the totems in an adult male's cultural system we may wonder whether his fanatic support of a local football team is more or less reasonable than the most extravagant adulation of a pop star, when it is commonly found in some areas that violence and absenteeism reflect success or failure of the football team. A man needs an interest, the 'folk' culture says. So do adolescents.

4 Adult Logic v. Adolescent Logic

One judges another person by one's own standards, his system of ideas by one's own systems. The other person's system of ideas is mediated linguistically through his participation in conversation, and much more rarely, though importantly, through his lectures or his monologues. Much of the logic of his systems, of the way his attitudes and opinions fit together is implied and virtually never made explicit (as in a written constitution). English sayings which illustrate this include 'There's no smoke without fire' (perceived causality), and euphemisms for courtship 'walking or going out (together)' (proximity).

But suppose a girl of the age that we have been considering spends time consistently over a considerable period with a particular boy. An initial conversation with a male adult revealing this fact will usually cause him to conclude that this boy is the titular boyfriend without further ado. He will be surprised if the girl refuses to confirm his conclusion. He may be refused because his cultural logic is incorrect, i.e. he has applied the logic of circumstances prevailing in his adult culture to a sample of circumstances from another sub-culture. This may seem a laborious way of putting it, but it does in fact account for innumerable British Forces Radio Network phone-in disc-jockey conversations I have heard in the last year in Germany between a disc-jockey and twelve to fourteen-year-old females telephoning a request for a particular person. It is always the case that the disc jockey jumps to conclusions about the relationship between the girl and the boy she requests a record for. And it is nearly always the case that it will be denied, or at best referred to ambiguously. In other words the adolescent maintains that the idea referred to (i.e. whether she is, for example, in 'love' with the boy) remain unanalysed. She may have good reasons for doing so. It may simply be an alliance of convenience, choice of companions often limited by size of family, childless neighbours, remote or isolated location, quite apart from personal considerations. So it is often the case that children accept a companion for no other reason than that he or she is more or less acceptable and available, knowing probably that when circumstances change the relationship will probably end.

The adult disc jockey tried to fit the boy–girl relationship referred to into his adult culture, with its 'adult' implications regarding sex and marriage. But he is often wrong in doing so. Later the same girl will admit readily to the implications of the disc jockey, and indeed these programmes are normally enjoyably suggestive.

Logic refers to a particular culture, set of objects and a set of attitudes towards these objects, and though these younger girls speak the same language as the disc-jockey, they are referring to a different cultural sub-system to his, and thus their logic is in this respect different. If their sub-culture and consequent logic differs from those of adults, then it is not surprising that their way of speaking evasively about objects in their culture such as pop idols reflects their different attitudes.

118

5 Language and Culture

I have spent a sizeable slice of my adult life looking at adolescents' conversation and I would like to explain some of my feelings about 'conversation' and its relation to 'culture'; and what I mean by both. I feel the necessity to do so since conversation is still an oddly neglected study despite its enormous presence in everyday life. This is perhaps because it is transitory and difficult to approach objectively. We are immersed in it and the 'distancing' effect necessary to 'study' anything is therefore difficult to achieve.

Conversation is the mechanism of social life, relating speakers to their social world, 'relating' in much the same way as the visual sense reduces discrepancies to apparent consistent order in the seen world, helps us to predict events, and makes the guesses without which the human nervous system works too slowly. So conversation relates us to social expectancies, to the stored knowledge of our language community and its social values. I have used the word culture frequently in this essay. I mean by it all those objects that may be referred to or implied by members of the native English speech community. By referring or implying, I mean as occurring in actual conversation. By sub-culture I mean in this case the sub-groups of this English community who habitually refer to, and attribute value to, a small group of 'objects' not so regarded by the community as a whole. So the whole community really means the adult culture and their objects, plus the adolescent sub-group where their 'objects' are shared with adults. By adolescent sub-group I mean with reference to those 'objects' which they share as a group, and which adults do not, or wish not to, share. Definitions of culture are notoriously legion, but I want to explain my meaning as used here.

ADOLESCENT CULTURE AND THE SECRET 'STOCK'

The collective topics of conversation of a group or a community or some such unity might be said to constitute the conversational cultural stock of that group, and could be referred to as the stock of common sense knowledge (or facts and attitudes), conversationally related to the systems of knowledge and beliefs existing or created in that group or community.

The topics of conversation likely to arise in conversations are nothing like so predictable as so-called high-frequency words. Indeed, less so, since such words are rarely counted according to their different senses, but simply as graphic symbols considered regardless of context. It means that the ability to operate in conversations depends to a great extent on the sum of knowledge that the speaker–hearer has of the language-specific culture of the participants. If you happen to be inexperienced in the culture of the language of the conversation, then you can only respond to those topics with which you have some experience or knowledge. The more predictable episodes of the ritual type in such cases have always seemed to me to be almost unbelievably understandable and predictable by contrast.

Much the same sort of thing, though not on anything like the same scale, is true of the thirteen to fifteen-year-old segment of the teenage 'culture' discussed in this essay. We as adults have very little knowledge of the cultural objects which at the present time bind together this adolescent community and I argue elsewhere that we have our own to concern ourselves with, and little time to study a community we think we already know. We have, then, little knowledge of the adolescents' present stock of conversational topics and exchanges which constitute the greater part of their common-sense knowledge of the world as interpreted by the community they live in, or as perceived by them.

We as adults simply do not see things the same way as this particular segment of the community, and I am tempted sometimes to make the analogy between the artist's reconstructions of bathrooms as perceived by children compared with adult perception of the same. Physical differences are much easier to understand, but for some parents the gap is, or seems to them at times to be, just as great between themselves and their children in their way of looking at things and talking about them. In fact adults 'know' more than most adolescents, about commonplace facts and interpretations of customs to do with jobs, approaching the opposite sex, and many other things. Adults are rarely in such unfamiliar situations as adolescents, and we most of us avoid the possibility since it can cause us embarrassment, but children are often forced into such situations in the name of social learning, or 'growing up'. The secret world of sex and sexual symbolism available to adolescents is a somewhat keyhole view by adult standards.

CLUB MEMBERSHIP

There is often an unspoken assumption on the part of most adults that since we were all 'that age' ourselves at one time that we are therefore ex-officio members of the 'club'. But club members have to obey the rules of the club, and membership requires consistent attendance, interest, and common aims. Adults are almost without exception members of a different club to the one so passionately adhered to by their teenage children, but they may like to think of themselves as founder members on occasions. It may well be resented because ex-officio membership of this particular club is not part of the 'constitution', in much the same way that children do not have automatic entrance to the adult 'club' without much pain and anguish.

6 Sampling and the Pop Model

WHY 'POP'?

Why pop stars? Because of the structured way I found they were talked about during six years of interviewing children and recording their conversations about their interests (see Rutherford, Freeth and Mercer 1969).

CONVERSATIONAL METHOD

Those of us working on the Child Language Survey did not use a standardized list of questions but tried to use simple conversational strategies to get a discussion going and then left the children or adolescents to it—to continue as and if they liked. We explained that we intended in no way to test them, and promised virtual anonymity to anything they said—removing the threat of authority as far as we could, substituting sympathetic-seeming adults (ourselves) for adults with authority. These would include any adult with sanction/punishment capacity such as almost any teacher, and all but the most saintly parents. It was always known, too, that we were only visitors for a short time in the school, which seemed to help both sides escape the consequences of anything that was said. Most children responded to the opportunity to talk about themselves, and their most frequent comment afterwards was that they had never talked to anyone (including their peers) about many of the topics they had in fact discussed. This caused some of them embarrassment when seen later in the school or in the neighbourhood with their friends. Most plainly enjoyed being specially picked out to be recorded. They had after all missed a lesson, which very few failed to appreciate. This was not necessarily a reflection on their teachers, more a welcome change in routine for most children.

Since we were wanting them to talk as freely as possible about their interests we thought of our own questions simply as leads—rather unrelated, though not entirely, to our own. It became a very obvious question arising in several different ways, to ask them about whether they liked pop music and if so anyone in particular. It generally arose out of finding that they spent time listening to the radio or to records. The question was generally answered without evasion. Either they were interested or they were not. What I found curious, as did anyone else who checked a tape against the transcript, was the invariable patience with which the children corrected and confirmed my mishearing and consequent mispronunciation of the names of the pop star or group they were currently interested in. I cannot think of more conclusive evidence of my ignorance of what they were talking about, but it was never a stumbling block to reasonably extensive discussion of the topic. It always seemed to be enough that an adult not in authority had asked the question neutrally—without implying in any way that the people referred to and their music were not worth talking about. For some parents, as for me, this is not difficult to do, but for many parents it is difficult, particularly if they feel their children are too interested in something which they feel is worthless, and cannot help either saying so or implying their feelings on the matter.

WHY THE POP QUESTION IS REVEALING

With pop music it has already been indicated that value judgements come into play. If adults are interested in pop music it is unlikely to be the same pop music as their children are interested in. It is more likely an interest in a singer who has satisfied them over a period of years, rather than the ephemeral successes represented by the Top Twenty charts, whose names are constantly changing and hence difficult for the adult to remember, are meant to represent the sales of records reflecting only top sellers, and ignore singers who make many records and whose records sell steadily rather than spectacularly. There are always exceptions, of course, where both parents and children for the most part share common interest in classical music. But even there, the children may 'betray' their adult tastes by showing enthusiasm for pop idols revered by their friends or associates, to the puzzlement of their parents. How can they (their children) be interested in such trash when they know and seem genuinely to feel for 'good' music? Adolescents rarely answer this question and evade it, usually avoiding attempts to analyse their interest. This process is described in section two as that of 'unanalysability'. This particular conflict of attitudes is discussed in section four on adult v. adolescent logic.

GENERAL STRUCTURE OF CONVERSATIONAL PANEGYRICS

Over the entire period of recording and collecting I found that the different age levels in a school provided me with 'keys' to easier conversation-making in the form of names of particular pop stars or groups, or types of music from a particular stable like 'Tamla Motown'. The keys were usually relevant to a particular age group, and the children themselves could confirm which 'keys' went with which age group or sub-group. I could and did check on this by asking more specific questions like: What do you think of A? (i.e. Donnie Osmond, Tamla Motown, etc.) This would produce the following kinds of responses: (a) An unanalysed panegyric (as in the Donnie Osmond transcript); (b) An explanation that A was relevant to a younger or older age group in the school, and that their age group key was different (and I could now ask about it); (c) A disclaimer—for example, that increased work for 'O' levels did not allow time for an *active* interest in pop, which was perhaps a similar sort of response as (b), but with a 'key' of a different kind; (d) A word-for-word recital of a current pop song.

This last was a common response in twelve to thirteen-year-old boys who had then (c. 1969) usually received a cheap record player, and who form a large part of the Top Twenty record buyers. They buy a few records in their first year of ownership and play them *ad nauseam*. Their choice of records is related primarily at this stage to the charts and only secondarily to the personality of the singers. Girls of this age group (immediately before the age group we are concerned with here) seemed able to mimic the words with ease, but their discussions were far more often revealing of general disillusionment, perhaps influenced by bodily changes.

POP PANEGYRICS

It is the unanalysed continuous and discontinuous pop panegyric which concerns me here, and all the concepts introduced refer to it, although I hope they can be generalized. By discontinuous, I mean, in the context of the Donnie Osmond transcript, a cyclical referring back to the topic of the singer once he has been

123

introduced, such that he seems to be relevant to almost any other topic discussed. There is nothing unusual in that. Most of us on occasion bring conversations round to the topic which pressingly occupies us, often regardless of any real link with the topic currently being discussed.

In general, I suspect that structurally all conversational pop panegyrics are similar, and that if you substitute the actual key names, the conversation will look much the same—unanalysed and unvaried. The only way, that the panegyric could be developed as in the transcript referred to, was to make references to it when talking about other topics, like the need to fill in certain chunks of free time in the school boarding routine in the evenings, or any other occasion when it was possible to listen to a record player.

SAMPLING

My ignorance of the particular pop 'key' referred to became a joke to those industrious ladies who typed our transcripts, and I often discussed the question with them since we occasionally had difficulty in identifying the name of a group that had later sunk to obscurity in the charts. In the last year of our work in York on the Child Language Survey, I asked my colleagues to help me identify a tape which particularly characterized the unanalysed topic structure I had so often noticed when actually making the recordings. The Donnie Osmond transcript eventually chosen was typical of many in its manner of discussing. It was dominated by discussions of the kind I wanted to illustrate, and was a tape of good technical quality. It was recorded in a girls' convent school in York, where a nun was perhaps over-zealous in taking an intelligent interest in the girls' conversations and interests. They were three intelligent, middle-class girls in the conversation, their ages between thirteen and a half and fifteen who knew well enough, I think, how to make the most of the obsession of one of their number with this singer, to the puzzled amazement of any adult curious enough to listen. The transcript was chosen, then, out of about 30 hours of conversation with this age group, and I hope provides the material for some hypotheses about an important bit of adolescent language and culture which may appeal to the intuition of those who have had dealings with this age group or are perhaps worth challenging.

I have not looked at syntax in this essay since testing hypotheses of a limited syntactic kind seems to me premature (as in so many current studies in child or adolescent language) without having looked first at the function of the language concerned, with the selection of cultural fronts which children struggle to make with remarkably little adult help at this stage. Very few adults asked to go through a similar struggle again in later life would do much better, in spite of having more knowledge of the world and its expectations. Unless read-made formulas will fit the new situation, then we suffer badly, as most exiles in their literature clearly reveal.

What do I mean by 'front' in this context? What sort of person does the adolescent want to be? What does he choose from? He sees his peers enthusing about pop. Can he afford not to? For one thing, his sense of diplomacy will warn him to conform, and another tells him it relates to an area of adult life, sex perhaps, which may be largely unexplored at first hand. The social and psychological pressures I have discussed in the section relating to adolescent culture.

And again, what do I mean about not looking narrowly at syntax before you have identified the function of the language you have collected? Briefly and grossly, I suppose you would not record the shouts of the crowd behind the goal at a German football match if you were looking for contextualized examples of the subjunctive in that language. Neither would you readily expect to find imperatives of that type that referees or players usually respond to on the football field, in the football column of a respectable newspaper. What has this to do with child language? Simply that in their conversations I am interested to discover their conversational strategies, the way they talk about what they want to discuss, and only very secondarily the complexity of the way they do, and then with a particular reason in mind. If I were to seek ways of training children to lecture on semantics and were to be interested to know what kind of language they might be expected to attain, then complexity of discourse would become a relevant matter of some rather academic educational interest to me, but I do not have this aim in mind for the children.

7 Application

Assuming my account of a small piece of adolescent behaviour is correct in spite of its generality, then what use is it? An account may be correct but without practical application. I hope this is not the case here.

In the first place, no teacher or mother will fail to notice such bits of unanalysed conversation going on in their presence from time to time. It can be profoundly annoying unless one realizes the function of such conversations is not that of communication-with-adults in general. Thus it is usually safe to be quite neutral about them. They will 'harm' you only if you allow them to annoy you. So simply understanding the function of such topics can help generally in dealing with adolescents, so long as you watch out for the potentially analysed topics where they are most anxious to come nearer or parrot adult views. These, for example, would include those topics where adults are repositories of needed information, often purely as the result of being old enough to have experience of the topics discussed. Examples of such topics might be public examinations, applying for university entrance, and the like, where it is unlikely that adolescents would have ready-made knowledge or experience of this segment of the adult world.

More actively, adults can partially participate in the adolescent culture by taking notice of the particular objects of sub-group totems (i.e. the selected pop figures), and avoiding irrelevant cultural condemnation. It is fashionable to overrate the significance of an oral tradition which was rapidly passing and is now undergoing a revival. Street cries, old broadsheets, rhymes and so on are carefully culled from learned sources with admirable scholarship and cutely presented with relevant paintings and photographs. There is nothing wrong with such interesting teaching material except that it implies an irrelevant value judgement about the cheap taste of many pop songs. Teachers are the kind of people to point out what seems to them best in what might be termed the English written culture. This is correct and adolescents expect it. But it is nevertheless an adult function which adolescents often feel is overdone. I mean for example the teacher who angrily urges his pupils to read a 'good' newspaper and himself reads a popular newspaper for most of his immediate needs since he is 'tired' or 'doesn't have time'. There is nothing wrong in getting your information the way lots of other people get it, providing you know why you do it and can assess it. In the same way it causes you unnecessary trouble with adolescents to condemn a current 'pop' idol without very good reason, since you have mistaken the function of their interest in the singer concerned. Better to use him, if you can: give an opinion, provided it is an honest one based on knowledge of one's own real interests and needs, different but often no 'better'. So if the preaching tone is not too indigestible, better to positively emphasize those values you believe in as a teacher and parent, than to condemn transitory adolescent totems which are not related to adult values. Finally, I don't believe it is at all necessary actually to 'like' a particular pop star currently obsessing your pupils or children. But you, and they, can at least talk about him, perhaps without analysing? It does not mean that you and they will not be able to develop critical insight using analytic language, but it can only be undertaken by discussing those topics which both the teacher and the adolescents are able to look at analytically.

Bibliography

BAC 14. Transcript of this conversation published in *Occasional Paper 64*, volume 1 (pp. 234–91) 'The Conversations of 14-year-old Children,' 1974. (Available from: MDU, Micklegate House, Micklegate, York, England. A tape should also be available.)

Rutherford, R. W., Freeth, M. E. A. and Mercer, E. S.: *Topics of Conversation in 15-year-old Children*, 1969, York. Also available from MDU.

Stoddart, Kenneth (1974), Pinched: Notes on the Ethnographer's Location of Argot'. In *Ethnomethodology Selected Readings*, ed. Turner, Roy, Penguin 1974.